PROPAGANDA
ESSENTIAL U2 QUOTATIONS

...urnalist ...d travel for ...*Times* and the *Irish* ...and *Connections* magazines. He has ...g other books, a biography of Elvis Costello and co-written a history of Irish rock music. He lives in County Meath with his wife Angela, and their two children, Paul and Sarah. His favourite U2 song is 'Kite'.

POPAGANDA

Essential U2 Quotations

Tony Clayton-Lea

Hodder Headline Ireland
8 Castlecourt Centre
Castleknock
Dublin 15
Ireland

A division of Hodder Headline
338 Euston Road, London NW1 3BH

HODDER
HEADLINE
IRELAND

...y Hodder Headline Ireland

The right of Tony Clayton-Lea to be identified as the Author of this Work has been asserted by him in accordance with the Copyright, Designs and Patents Act 1988.

1

A CIP catalogue record for this title is available from the British Library.

ISBN 978 0340 93353 4

Typeset in Georgia, Berlin and Schindler by Hodder Headline Ireland

Printed and bound in Great Britain by Clays Ltd, St Ives plc.

Contents

To the women in my life and the life in my women:
Angela, May and Sarah.

Introduction

Opinions of U2 are like a certain part of the anatomy – everybody has one. Indifference isn't an option when it comes to what is arguably the Biggest Rock Band In The World. Just because they're big, however, doesn't necessarily mean that they're the best – and that isn't at opinion, by the way, merely an observation. Besides, as everyone except fans of pornography will tell you, size doesn't matter. What matters, essentially, is what U2 mean to people. If you're not a fan or haven't got a bull's notion about the validity of rock music as a means of communication then, clearly, you are holding this book under false pretences. If you are a fan or have some idea of how important music can be to bridge the gap between the head, heart, the soul and the groin, then you'll know that, on more than several occasions, U2 hit the bullseye.

It wasn't always the case. In the late 1970s, U2 could barely hit the dart board. They also didn't have the critics on their side. The more acerbic arbiters of taste of the period disliked U2's notions of themselves, and considered the band artificial and brash. In point of fact, U2 existed beyond the restrictive Dublin music scene and its clique, having crucial allies in the likes of (then) burgeoning manager Paul McGuinness and (then) fledgling music magazine *Hot Press*. Their personal backgrounds, also – two members Catholic, two Protestant, two Irish, two English by birth;

Mount Temple was Ireland's first comprehensive, co-educational and multi-denominational school – made them distinctive by nature if not by inclination. This difference was made all the more divisive by the growing involvement of the band (with the exception of Adam Clayton) in Born Again Christianity – notably with the Shalom Bible group, whose theme of ego-less self-surrender would remain a lifestyle motif for some time.

Throughout the past thirty years, they have made several transitory journeys, shedding skin (but never members) along the way. For the past twenty years, they have hung on to the title of Biggest Rock Band In The World, while lead singer Bono has become as familiar with statesmen as he has with stagehands. Some years have been shaky – competing bands arrived, had a good look around, reaped the dividends while U2 were in recording studios working on their next album, and departed – but, overall, it's fair to say that no single band has ever come close to stealing U2's crown. Sometime soon they will release a new album, their third of this decade, and will no doubt add another gazillion sales to the already preposterously large number of records they have sold. No solo albums yet, then.

In the meantime, here they are, mostly in their own words – at which you just might smile, smirk, sneer, agree/disagree, nod sagely or throw your eyes up to heaven. From baby band to founding fathers of modern arena rock, from Adam Clayton's flagrant Full Montys to Bono's strategically placed semi-colons, here are thirty years of words, snippets, soundbites and life sentences.

Tony Clayton-Lea
April 2007

Sex and Sexuality

Sex, sexy, sexuality – they mean different things to different people (it's all in the eye of the beholder, apparently) but would it be fair to say that until Bono started wearing those 'Fly' shades and making love with a videocam that he wasn't remotely sexy? Edge, meanwhile, is far too much of a technically minded intellectual to be ever considered sexy. Adam will show off parts of his body at the drop of a frilly sombrero, but is that sexy or just plain narcissistic? Larry? Well, everyone knows that from the early days, it was Larry that the girls understood. Even now, well into his forties, Larry has the unerring ability to cause normally tight-lipped adult women (and men – let's not forget his status in the gay community) to drool uncontrollably and forget about their responsibilities. Is that sexy? With knobs on.

'If you can't pull tonight, you're hopeless.'

Adam Clayton, at the video shoot soiree for 'One' at Nell's Manhattan nightclub, attended by straights, gays and drag queens, in Bill Flanagan, *U2 at the End of the World* (1995).

'It is a love song. In a sense, it's an attempt to write about a woman in a spiritual sense and about God in a sexual sense. But there certainly is a strong sexual pulse in there.'

Bono, on 'Gloria', in Visnja Cogan, *U2 – an Irish Phenomenon* (2006).

'He's a rampant sex god with a huge ego.'

Edge, on Bono, *The Face* (April 1992).

'And a small willy.'

Adam Clayton adds, *The Face* (April 1992).

'Once you take alcohol out of the equation, there's a lot less sex.'

Adam Clayton, *Q* (November 2004).

'I don't know why, but I'm always attracted to subjects that you can't really get a grip on, like sex or God. I think I sometimes confuse them both.'

Bono on Bono (2005).

'Fidelity is just against human nature. That's where we have to either engage or not engage our higher side … It's like in school when they tell you about drugs – "If you smoke drugs you'll become an addict and you'll die the next week." They don't tell you even half the truth. I think the same is true about sex. You know, if you tell people that the best place to have sex is in the safe hands of a loving relationship, you may be telling a lie! There may be other places. If the question is: Can I as a married man write about sex with a stranger? Then has got to be the answer. I've got to write about that because that is part of the subject I'm writing about. You have to try and expose some myths, even if they expose you along the way. I don't want to talk about my own relationship, because I've too much respect for Ali to do so. What I'm saying to you is, I may or may not be writing from my own experience on some of these, but that doesn't make it any less real.'

Bono, in Bill Flanagan, *U2 at the End of the World* (1995).

Adam: 'I'd have to say that within the U2 camp, I would definitely be the most diminutive of all the members.'

Edge: 'Adam is the most well-endowed member, no contest, but he wouldn't know because he's blind.'

Bono: 'Some people think U2 should be hung. All I am saying is that we are, in fact, particularly well hung.'

Locker room chat, in *U2 By U2* (2006).

'You probably wanted it to be about a waitress.'

Bono, on 'Gloria', in John Waters, *Race of Angels – the Genesis of U2* (1994).

'I don't think I know many women who are tarts, but I know a lot of men.'

Bono, in Niall Stokes, *Into the Heart: The Stories behind Every U2 Song* (2001).

'The funny thing about Larry was that, okay, he got into the dress and he put on make-up, but he was fighting with it. He wouldn't take off his Doc Martens and when he was sitting he'd put his feet up on the table. But as macho as he tried to be, he still looked like some extra from a skin flick ... Whereas Adam was just getting people to do him up in the back and swapping make-up tips with any girl that passed. You know, suddenly he could own up to being interested in their underwear.'

Bono, on Larry Mullen Jr's initial reaction on the 'One' drag-queen video shoot, in Bill Flanagan, *U2 at the End of the World* (1995).

'All my mother's side of the family have that taxi-driver-from-Tel-Aviv look.'

Bono on Bono (2005).

'Am I a massive shagger? Of course I am. You should ask the missus. People are sometimes surprised that I am such a flirt but I've never met a halfway good performer who isn't ... I like the company of women.'

Bono, *Q* (January 2006).

Interviewer: 'What is your most treasured possession?'
Adam: 'My willy!'

Adam Clayton, *ZooTV Tour Programme* (1992).

'I want to fuck you!'

Female fan to Bono, in Hershey, Pennsylvania, in B.P. Fallon, *U2 Faraway So Close* (1994).

'I had fun flirting with Christy, but I never had an affair with her! I wouldn't. After introducing these beautiful women to my wife, they lost all interest in me! They're her friends now.'

Bono, on tabloid tittle-tattle about him and supermodel Christy Turlington, in Bill Flanagan, *U2 at the End of the World* (1995).

'Gay clubs are the best place for us to come to. Nobody hassles you, there's not the asshole you find in other clubs who just has to get up and try to start something. They respect us and they're glad to have us. The gay community is always on the cutting edge in music. I'm proud that they like U2 and come to our concerts. They don't see in U2 that macho shit that's beneath so much rock. I have a lot of time for the gay community.'

Larry Mullen Jr, in Bill Flanagan, *U2 at the End of the World* (1995).

'I love women, they're definitely the stronger sex. Some of my best friends are women. Some of my best friends dress up as women, too.'

Bono, *Hot Press* (December 1988).

'Rhythm is the sex of music. If U2 is to explore erotic themes, we have to have sexuality in the music as well as the words.'

Bono, in Bill Flanagan, *U2 at the End of the World* (1995).

Interviewer: 'Do you ever wish you were a woman?'

Adam: 'Yeah, I think I'd be a much better woman than I am a man. I think my talents are more in that direction. I don't mind dressing up, I don't think it makes much difference, not really. I'd love to wear women's underwear if the sizes were right, but they don't really support you, you just tend to flop one way or the other.'

Larry: 'I never even thought about it to be honest with you.'

Edge: 'I wondered what it would be like, more than wished I was. I'm still fascinated by what it would be like, yeah, and just their minds, the way they think, ooh...'

Bono: 'When we did the drag shoot, Edge looked like Winnie The Witch, Adam looked like the Duchess Of York ... and I looked like ... Barbara Bush.'

ZooTV Tour Programme (1992).

Drugs and Alcohol

Known as a Christian rock band for the best part of ten years – from their debut *Boy* to late 1980s album *Rattle And Hum* – U2's image as an archetypal rock 'n' roll band suffered in the fallout of the more religious/spiritual aspects of their songs and lifestyle. The sole member of the band who took wholeheartedly to the drink and the drugs was the one who didn't espouse the Christian way of life – Adam. Such habits, however, have a way of biting one on the backside, which is what happened to the bass player in the early 1990s when, because of too many glasses of after-dinner sherry, he missed an important gig in Australia. These days, Adam leads an alcohol-free lifestyle. The rest of the band know how to party, mind – although because of the way the grape affects his system, Bono can now only drink vintage wine. It's a tough job ...

'Adam didn't have any partners in crime in the band, so some of the people he ended up hanging out with were dodgy – road warriors who had been around the block ... I mean, the band weren't even drinking. Can you imagine?! You're in a candy store and these guys don't even want to smell the sweets. Strange days indeed.'

Larry Mullen Jr, in *U2 By U2* (2006).

'It's one of those personal experiences that you wish the rest of the world didn't necessarily get involved in, because it's got nothing to do with the music. Nowadays, the number of people who quietly have a joint at the end of their day is a very large proportion of the population. So it's like a bit of a reality check – OK, you may live a lifestyle that is reasonably relaxed, but it's still illegal and it's illegal for an awful lot of people. You can't fuck with that aspect of the society you live in … for better or for worse.'

Adam Clayton, *Q* (March 1997).

'There were drugs being consumed openly, lines of cocaine on mirrors in our dressing rooms. I had no experience of drugs and judging by the people offering them to me, it was an experience I could do without.'

Larry Mullen Jr, in *U2 By U2* (2006).

'Bottom line: I think drugs are dumb. Bottom line: I think abuse of alcohol is dumb. Bottom line: I think that cigarette smoking is dumb. And that's it, really.'

Bono on Bono (2005).

'It was a disappointment and a wake-up call.'

Paul McGuinness, on Adam Clayton's no-show, in *U2 By U2* (2006).

'It was a moment. We just thought, OK, this guy's having a problem, let's just see what we can do. That was first and foremost and what we did afterwards is between ourselves ... It was an unfortunate thing. But it doesn't come up in conversation – it's not something we talk about generally.'

Larry Mullen Jr, on Adam Clayton's no-show in Sydney in December 1993, *Q* (March 1997).

'It was a moment where I had to face a lot of things I hadn't really been facing and realise that if I was going to be able to go on and be a useful member of this band I had to beat alcohol. I had to realise that every fuck-up of mine, every problem over the last ten years that hasn't been quite so serious as that night, has been related to alcohol abuse.'

Adam Clayton, on his no-show in Sydney, in Bill Flanagan, *U2 at the End of the World* (1995).

'The real betrayal in Sydney was not between Adam and the band. The real betrayal was between Adam and himself, because there is no more pro a person in the band than Adam. He found it very hard to live with that ... It took him a few years, but that was a real turning point.'

Bono on Bono (2005).

'They were pretty concerned and a bit pissed off as well. But they supported me in the decision that I made at that time, which was to say to them that I had a problem with alcohol. It was then that I officially stopped drinking.'

Adam Clayton, on his no-show at Sydney's Football Stadium (26 November 1993), in *U2 By U2* (2006).

'In its simplest form, I've always seen heroin as a very evil thing. Consequently, that's always inspired a great fear of it in me, so I can assume that anyone who takes it has a similar fear. To actually have their back so much against the wall, to be controlled by it, is something I can't understand. I haven't been that close to the edge. I've certainly been near it a few times in one way or another, but to imagine that next stage is pretty much impossible.'

Adam Clayton, *Hot Press* (March 1987).

'I find them much easier, actually. You can avoid the pitfalls. I think the pitfalls are being the last person in the bar.'

Adam Clayton, on attending music-industry events – sober, *Q* (December 2004).

'We were in a very different orbit. Drugs, sex, you had a sense occasionally that they were there but they just weren't a part of our world. We met, really, the best people. And the worst you could say about them was they were wearing silk jackets with radio stations' numbers on their backs.'

Bono, in *U2 By U2* (2006).

'Me?! No, I don't ... I, I, I'll ... y'know ... but um, it's not my thing. In a way, I find that the colours are already quite bright for me.'

Bono, when asked if he smoked joints, *Q* (March 1997).

'There are very few things, I would imagine, that can rival the high of heroin for people looking for a way out of a low life ... It was my faith that brought me ...'

Bono, *Hot Press* (December 1988).

'I developed a taste for whisky. Whisky does not make me sleepy, unlike wine which I drink now, so I didn't want to go to bed. I'd be swinging out of the rafters. I could drink a lot of it and it didn't seem to make me drunk but I was thumping the odd punter, so I put that away. "Oh gosh, the bloke that wrote the song about Martin Luther King, is that the bloke that just tried to break my nose?" I put a stop to that.'

Bono, recalling the *Rattle And Hum* Los Angeles period, in *U2 By U2* (2006).

'I wasn't really in control, it would be fair to say. Every night was a party, but I don't think I felt much contentment or peace, that's for sure. I'd be fine during the day, I'd be fine for the gig but afterwards it was too easy to go out all night or just keep drinking in your room. I was beginning to realise that every time I drank, I couldn't really be sure of the result. And it always made the next day worse.'

Adam Clayton, in *U2 By U2* (2006).

'It was my idea to relocate to New York ... and start a new life as a non-drinker, which is commonly known as 'doing the geographic'. It was surprisingly easy to stop, but it was difficult to stay stopped. I ended up smoking a lot of marijuana, which is not exactly a solution. It stops you getting drunk, but it stops you doing just about anything else.'

Adam Clayton, in *U2 By U2* (2006).

The Rock 'n' Roll Lifestyle

Adam recalls that, from the early days of touring, he'd be up in the front of the bus swigging beer and smoking jazzy coffin nails while the remainder of the band gathered at the back to read passages from the Bible. Come the 1990s, *Achtung Baby, ZooTV* and *Pop*, it was mostly all change – out went the image of the puritanical Pale Riders, in came supermodels, tabloid media coverage, synapse-blitzing rock 'n' roll imagery, arch, ironic and witty soundbites and a touring lifestyle of the super-rich. With a reinvention of their sound and image from the 1990s onwards, U2 gave themselves a new lease of life. It's almost impossible to imagine what they were like prior to this radical makeover – their music reflected their personalities like few other arena rock bands: very worthy, earnest, moderately exciting but mired in a style that entrapped them. Now? Rock stars from head to toe embracing the lifestyle when it suits them.

Interviewer: 'What turned you on to rock 'n' roll?'

Bono: 'There were a few incidents – seeing Elvis, seeing Tom Jones – yeah! – and realising I fancied Marc Bolan and he wasn't a girl and I thought this rock 'n' roll was quite a potion if it can do that to me cos I'm very heterosexual.'

Bono, *ZooTV Tour Programme* (1992).

'Being a rock & roll star is like having a sex change! People treat you like a girl! ... They stare at you, they follow you down the street, they hustle you. And then they try to fuck you over! It's a hard thing to talk about because it's so absurd, but actually it's valuable. When I'm with women, I know what it feels like. I know what it feels like to be a babe.'

Bono, in Bill Flanagan, *U2 at the End of the World* (1995).

'I went out every night and stayed out all night, which was something I had never done before and haven't done since ... I also went off on my own, which I hadn't done before either. I found myself in all kinds of weird and wonderful situations, and though I avoided getting into serious trouble, I did get into some. I had become so used to being away from home, so caught up in U2 world, the idea of coming back to any form of normality was making me nervous. I didn't know if I was ready to go back to Dublin and sleep in my own bed and get up and deal with my family and friends. Normal life looked alien to me.'

Larry Mullen Jr, on Zooropa's visit to Tokyo, in *U2 By U2* (2006).

'On the road, you enter this twilight zone, this other reality, and you get home and all this time's gone by. For you, it seems like you just left. For everyone else, all this stuff's been happening. You do lose a chunk of your life. But there's other massive compensations. We're very lucky, we have the opportunity to bring our friends and family out from time to time ... So it's not like it used to be in the early days when you'd go on the road and you literally wouldn't see anyone for two or three months. That was more difficult. But then, that was about survival. This isn't really about survival – this is about doing great work.'

Edge, *Mojo* (July 2005).

'I don't think it's real at all. I think it's great fun, it's a little bit like when you were a kid and you played at dressing up, it still has that quality to it. Mind you, it does have a reality of its own because you move in a world that you're still familiar and comfortable with, but it's still different to when you go home and water your cabbages.'

Adam Clayton, in B.P. Fallon, *U2 Faraway So Close* (1994).

'We've gotten better at being rock stars; that's something I'm not sure we should be proud of. We got good at insincerity, but only to protect ourselves, to be able to continue to be sincere in our work.'

Bono on Bono (2005).

'Death to whinging rock stars, their miserable entourages and their ten bodyguards. I never needed a security guy. I had one on the road once because there were some death threats at the time and he was taking his job seriously, but I used to sneak away from him, get offside ... You go out onto the streets of Chicago with two giants and people are gonna

start paying attention. I avoid that stuff and as a result I have much more fun than your regular rock star.'
Bono, *Q* (February 2002).

'For a while Bono was Bon Smelly Arse. I was glad that didn't stick, or things might have been different. I don't know if the band could have got very far with a singer called Bon Smelly Arse.'
Edge, on early band-member nicknames, in *U2 By U2* (2006).

'The night after Bernie Melman's party, they were listening to WINS news radio for progress reports on the beached whale as they motored slowly towards the city. By eleven, it was pronounced dead. The music stations, meanwhile, all played the same lugubrious U2 songs over and over – 'With or Without You' and 'I Still Haven't Found What I'm Looking For', real Save the Whales music. Phil Collins was bound to whine into earshot any minute now. It seemed to Corrine that rock and roll was more fun when they had first come to New York, when they used to stay out half the night dancing. Whatever happened to Blondie, the Cars, The Clash?'
Jay McInerney, *Brightness Falls* (1992).

'May I say without guile, I am as sick of messianic rock stars as the next man, woman and child.'
Bono, *The Independent* (16 May 2006).

'We've always felt very uncomfortable around men who are part of that rock & roll culture, that macho thing. A lot of men in rock and roll tend to be over-dramatic. They act like queens, regardless of their heterosexuality. They seem to be hysterical, rather than just happy to work away at something. And I think it's a need for female contact within our world.'

Adam Clayton, on the number of women working in the Principle Management offices, in Bill Flanagan, *U2 at the End of the World* (1995).

'U2 party like no one else: they have the stamina of fourteen-year-old kids. But a lot of the time at those parties, everybody would be going to bed and it would be just us and their wives left sitting up.'

Helena Christensen, supermodel, on U2's party habits, *Q* (November 2002).

'I think rock 'n' roll has more contradictions than any other art form. Whether it's been art and commerce, idealism or nihilism, it goes on and on – a fuzzbox versus a gospel choir.'

Bono, *NME* (13 June 1992).

'We're pretending to know it all. People say that rock 'n' roll shouldn't be about religion and spirituality, shouldn't be political. Well, I disagree.'

Edge, *Q* (August 2006).

Interviewer: 'What do you plan to do after the tour ends?'

Bono: 'Extend the tour ... reality isn't what it's cracked up to be.'

Bono, *ZooTV Tour Programme* (1992).

'It was kind of weird going back to houses at night because there was no room service. I preferred staying in hotels.'

Adam Clayton, on the band decamping nightly to the Hamptons during the Rattle And Hum tour, in *U2 By U2* (2006).

'While there were times when you might need escorts to get in and out of gigs, usually it was done very discreetly. Now, we were allowing the press to see it, and basically saying, "Yeah, we are rock stars, we have police escorts, we travel around in limousines and, you know what, we're not embarrassed about it any more." There were certain things that made me cringe but there was something refreshing about saying, "Yeah, this is the shit, this is what goes on, and it's a lot of fun." The honesty was a huge relief ... People thought we had abandoned the past. Really, we had abandoned our own insecurities.'

Larry Mullen Jr, on the *Achtung Baby* phase, in *U2 by U2* (2006).

'It suits us that people believe we're choirboys, cos it means we can get away with murder.'

Larry Mullen Jr, *Mojo* (July 2005).

'The loss of my mother definitely started me singing and writing, but the audience was probably some sort of attempt at my father. It goes without saying, if we were completely of sound mind and proportion in our thinking, we wouldn't be performers.'

Bono, *The Independent* (16 May 2006).

'They've never been a kind of big classic rock act – it's not sex, drugs, rock and roll, girls backstage, and all that sort of stuff. They're very low key. They like to party, but it's perfectly innocent. I guess that comes from self-confidence as well: you don't need to live that life in order to be serious about what you're doing, and they've always been serious.

They've changed in their presentation, but the message is the same. They're serious about being ironic. They're serious about taking the piss out of themselves and everything around them. They take their music and their business seriously, and it's to their credit that they've never let any of that slip. They're on top of it, they're interested, they're engaged, they're involved and nothing really happens regarding them as a brand, an entity, a unit and as a band that they're not fully conversant with and happy about. So, is that rock and roll? Probably not. It's more like big business.'

Ned O'Hanlon, film producer, in Diana Scrimgeour, *U2 Show* (2004).

'We owe a lot of our good taste to Paul [McGuinness], who would rather starve than not eat in a Michelin-rated restaurant. From hanging around him, I knew more about wine than amplifiers when I was twenty.'

Bono, *Vanity Fair* (November 2004).

'That whole supermodel, club-going, paparazzi thing was not really my scene. I found it a little uncomfortable. They were all nice people and I was very fond of them, but some people don't do Christmas, some people don't like beaches, some people don't like the wind, some people don't like the sun. The fashion world is not my natural habitat.'

Larry Mullen Jr, in *U2 By U2* (2006).

'Rock 'n' roll is a spirit, it's not just about a style of playing guitar. When we talk about rock 'n' roll, we're not gonna suddenly turn into Bon Jovi.'

Edge, *Q* (March 1997).

'Rock 'n' roll is obsessed with juvenilia and skinny boys, which is cool, and I understand the homoerotic implications of that. But with wasted young men, you smile rather than pull back, and with a lot of these older groups you just want to wrestle them to the ground and cut their hair and stop this sixteen-year-old thing. Because there's something about knowing who you are and where you are.'

Bono, Q (March 1997).

'It's a world within a world and when you stop and try to get off it's weird. Sometimes, I find myself at home and someone says, "Would you mind moving that?" And I say, "Surely somebody else should be doing this?" "No, it's your house." It's a mad thing we do. There's nothing natural about it. I mean, I hit things for a living ... and people clap!'

Larry Mullen Jr, on touring, Q (July 2001).

'As much as we need to describe the kind of world we live in, we need to dream up the kind of world we want to live in. In the case of a rock 'n' roll band that is to dream out loud, at high volume ... Rock and roll is for some of us a kind of alarm clock. It wakes us up to dream!'

Bono, speaking at an anti-fascist event at Thalia Theatre, Hamburg (1993).

'U2 have made their own course. They're not like anybody else I know ... Anybody who works with them will tell you that they're the most honorable, extraordinary people. All of them. Normally with bands, the more you get into it, the more rotten the core is in many cases. This guy's wife hates that guy, and the other guy's wife, etc. They're at each other's throats and everything collapses. With U2, they're just solid

... They've never lost their heads through all this. Always kept their feet on the ground. Never lost their roots. Just regular people. Believe me, it's more than unusual.'

Chris Blackwell, founder of Island Records, in Diana Scrimgeour, *U2 Show* (2004).

'I don't think people see me or U2 as, like, "Ooh, rock stars!" They see us like themselves, despite the rarified air of some of our dwellings.'

Bono, *Q* (January 2006).

'I'm not built for the schmooze. I'm not good at small talk. I've got about one hand of friends and a few acquaintances. I'm cautious by nature and I don't like bullshit, so that doesn't bode well for being in a band.'

Larry Mullen Jr, *Q* (July 2001).

'The rock star I put together for myself [for ZooTV] was an identikit. I had Elvis Presley's leather jacket, Jim Morrison's leather pants, Lou Reed's fly shades, Jerry Lee Lewis's boots, Gene Vincent's limp. You want rock 'n' roll stuff? I'll give you some.'

Bono on Bono (2005).

'If rock 'n' roll means anything it's liberation, it's freedom.'

Bono on Bono (2005).

'The lifestyle that goes with touring? Touring is completely mad, completely unnatural, completely false, and when you do it for long periods of time ... you tend to get used to it, which is worse. It just means that when you go home you feel like you've just gone to Mars because normality seems so weird.'

Edge, in B.P. Fallon, *U2 Faraway So Close* (1994).

'Never trust a performer, performers are always the best liars. They lie for a living.'

Bono on Bono (2005).

Interviewer: 'What is the worst thing about touring?'

Edge: 'Apart from having to leave behind all the people you love, the worst thing about touring is coming home and spending two months of cold turkey trying to pick up the threads of your life that you had before you left. That's hard cos you spend a long time finding normal life very weird, and the first few mornings you wake up and reach for the telephone to order room service breakfast and you realise you are in your house and you wonder why there is no CNN on the television and shit like that. And people ask you weird questions like, pass the salt, and round 7.00 o'clock you start getting very fidgety, you realise there is no show. Strange things happen, like certain pieces of music you've used as intro tapes ... you're at home and somebody puts that on the record player and you suddenly start crawling up the walls, the adrenalin starts going. It's like this Pavlov's Dog reaction. There's a song called '4th of July' that we used to use all the time, and I still can't hear it without thinking we're about to do a show.'

Edge, *ZooTV Tour Programme* (1992).

'I can't even begin to describe the feeling of what it is to be part of something like the U2 thing on the road, on every level. All the fun of the circus. Renting a couple of 747s and just, y'know, crashing them.'

Bono, *Q* (March 1997).

'I think I've gotten better at it over the last few years, but I don't think I'm very good at it ... [People like] Michael Stipe ... Liam Gallagher ... [are] more comfortable with it. I've gotten more comfortable with it but I don't really believe in the role. Some people make something of the role and have some fun with it. For me, after years of trying to dodge it, I've found a way of playing with it ... And those Fly shades – they worked a treat, they really did.'

Bono, on being a rock star, *Q* (February 1998).

'There was no uniform policy at school and I think there had been some talk about whether a boy could get away with wearing a skirt. As I had become a smoker, money was increasingly important because then you could buy cigarettes ... So I had persuaded a number of people to bet me fifty pence each that I wouldn't wear a skirt in school.'

Adam Clayton, in *U2 By U2* (2006).

'This soap opera of people setting fire to themselves – my objection is that we don't get to hear their second, third, fourth album. Fretting over people torturing themselves? I'm over it.'

Bono, *Cara* (June 2005).

'We always add a week to the end of a tour where we stay in a hotel. It was my wife Ali's idea – "Take a week, love, because I don't want the kids to see you like this." And I know the aftermath is where people come apart. I know

Keith Richards started doing drugs not on tour but when he came off tour, cos there was such a big hole in his life.'

Bono, *Q* (February 2002).

'You find yourself on the dinner table, maniacally swinging a lightbulb, telling jokes that aren't funny.'

Bono, on being asked what he's like when he arrives home after being on the road, *Vanity Fair* (November 2004).

'One of the good things about being in a rock 'n' roll band, and a successful band, is that you don't have to think too far into the future, you can pretty much make it up as you go along. And that gives you control over your own destiny, which is a very rare thing in the world today. We could break up ... we could do another album, go on the road again, whatever. It's simply about the consensus of the four members of the group ... Maybe we won't tour for another ten years. That's why I'm in a rock 'n' roll band and not working in a bank. I like that freedom.'

Edge, in B.P. Fallon, *U2 Faraway So Close* (1994).

'Some people back in Dublin say these shows remind them of our earliest shows back in the late 1970s, in the spirit of them, the mischief. I believe that rock 'n' roll is about mystery and mischief. And in the 1980s we weren't being a rock 'n' roll band, we were just a very, very loud folk group. But we're definitely a rock 'n' roll band again now.'

Bono, *Q* (January 1993).

'We're not really believable as rock 'n' roll stars, though we've gotten much better at it.'

Bono on Bono (2005).

'When you come off a tour, you should be given the kind of warning a doctor gives his patient after prescribing Valium: don't take any important decisions or drive a car for a while.'
Paul McGuinness, in *U2 By U2* (2006).

'I love Middle Eastern women. I think they're very mysterious and I think that in the West people have a really corny attitude to sex and it's very obvious. I like the veiled attitude of Middle Eastern women. Arabic women have been very badly mistreated over the years, but despite that they have real grace. And grace is the thing I love best in anybody. I find them very sexy. It's a very un-American kinda sexuality in that it's not *Playboy*, it's not tits and ass, it's not so skinny as European sexuality. It's playful, it's mischievous but it has mystery – like rock 'n' roll should be.'
Bono, in B.P. Fallon, *U2 Faraway So Close* (1994).

'Sam Shepard said, "Right in the centre of contradiction, that's the place to be." And rock and roll has more contradictions than any art form. U2 spent the 1980s trying to resolve some of them. Now we've started the 1990s celebrating them. Rock and roll is ridiculous. It's absurd. In the past, U2 was trying to duck that. Now we're wrapping our arms around it and giving it a great big kiss. It's like I say on stage, "Some of this bullshit is pretty cool."'
Bono, *Rolling Stone* (1 October 1992).

Interviewer: 'Are you a star?'

Bono: 'No, a firework ... Well more of a banger, really.'
Bono, *ZooTV Tour Programme* (1992).

Religion and Spirituality

Let's not be cynical about this point – overt spirituality and some kind of religious yearning permeates pretty much everything U2 have done. From the mindset behind their debut album *Boy* and its follow-up, *October*, right through to their 2004 album *How To Dismantle An Atomic Bomb* – not forgetting the celebratory communality of their appearance at Live Aid; indeed, most if not all of their concerts – U2 have embraced their God so close to the collective heart that it sometimes seems as if there is almost no space left for anything else. Interestingly, it hasn't detracted from their popularity, which surely has as much to do with the music as with the band's personality. Humour is a saving grace, of course; charm, too. To their advantage, U2 are able to naturally blend the two with a trenchant belief system (equal parts deep-rooted humanitarianism and deft rock 'n' roll ripostes) that seems now to be virtually unassailable.

'Best to be upfront about these things. I am one. Isn't everyone?'

Bono, on why he has the word 'sinner' stencilled on one of his leather jackets, *Q* (January 2006).

'The prayer meetings were a safe haven because they brought us together through some of the ups and downs of being on the road ... There were many things that we didn't feel right about doing. Looking back now, it was very extreme and led me to misjudge too many situations. We were learning to distance ourselves, we were training to be separatists.'

Larry Mullen Jr, *U2 By U2* (2006).

'We're all members of the Frisbeetarian Order ... We believe that when you die your soul goes up on a roof and you can't get it down.'

Bono, *Hot Press* (June 1987).

'Call to me and I will answer you and will tell you great and hidden things which you have not known.'

The Bible [Jeremiah, chapter 33, verse 3], quoted on the cover of *All That You Can't Leave Behind* where U2 are seen hanging around an airport terminal and the departure gate sign reads J33-3. Quoted in *Q Special Edition: The 150 Greatest Rock Lists Ever* (2004).

'In the post-punk wastelands of the 1970s/early 1980s, U2 were impossibly idealistic, striving for deliverance through the healing power of music – rock 'n' roll as nothing short of spiritual transcendence.'

Sean O'Hagan, *NME* (19 December 1987).

'I have to accept that one of the things that I picked up from my father and my mother was the sense that religion often gets in the way of God.'

Bono on Bono (2005).

'I couldn't let go of my faith. But what's more interesting is that I don't think God will let go of me. I love it when people on bar stools rub their chins and say, "Do you believe in God?" That's so presumptuous. A much more important question is, "Does God believe in us?"'

Bono, *Q* (January 2006).

'I've never believed that this is God's world, anyway. I always thought that this was our world, and that we are the ones to hold to account, not religion. There's enough food to go around, but we don't share it. There's enough medicine around, but it's too expensive. We could turn every desert into fertile land, but we don't. It is human beings that need to be held to account, not God.'

Bono, *Hot Press Yearbook* (2002).

'It's not me, it's not U2 that's creating this great art. That's why I can be so arrogant or seemingly arrogant about what we do because I don't believe it's us. Essentially, I think there's something that works through us to create in this way.'

Edge, in Barry Devlin (director) *The Making of The Unforgettable Fire Video* (1985).

'I reject religion, the idea of religion, when it creates conflict between two people. There is a confusion between religion and spirituality. Music has always been spiritual.'

Bono, *Best* (October 1984).

'One thing I think people forget is how radical Christ was. People were put to death for the idea that all men were created equal, which meant essentially that Jewish peasants were equal to Roman emperors. That was radical. And to me, there's nothing more radical or revolutionary than love – the love two people have for each other, for instance. Because it's so hard to find. My version of love is not soft, it's hard. You know, the Christ I read about in the gospels is steel not straw.'

Bono, *Hot Press* (December 1988).

'I think it's possible to be spiritual without sacrificing your credibility. Look at U2 – they touched on those issues in a way that was tasteful and positive.'

Brandon Flowers, lead singer with The Killers, *Hot Press* (4 October 2006).

'All I do is get up on the Cross of the Ego: the bad hangover, the bad review. When I look at the Cross of Christ, what I see up there is all my shit and everybody else's.'

Bono on Bono (2005).

'It's the blues of the Bible.'

Bono, in his introduction to the Pocket Canon edition of the Book of Psalms, *The Irish Times* (2006).

'"Love Thy Neighbour" is a command, not a piece of advice.'

Bono, *The Observer* (21 May 2006).

'There have never been any rules applied to my faith. My faith is a personal thing. I'm sure there are things you can get away with like anything else, and there's no doubt that we push it to the edge. And occasionally we fall off the other end.

But I never felt my job as a musician was to sing gospel or proselytize. I've always felt that I'm a musician in a band and I've been given a gift. And I believe that gift is from God. I don't believe it's from anywhere else. And if at any stage I abuse that, I think I'll know. That will be time to stop.'

Larry Mullen Jr, in Bill Flanagan, *U2 at the End of the World* (1995).

'Religion can be the enemy of God. It's often what happens when God, like Elvis, has left the building.'

Bono on Bono (2005).

'They were often misquoted and felt used and abused. The evangelical Christian world seemed to claim U2 as its property, and therefore U2's members found their faith defined and explained by magazines rather than by the members themselves. Aligning themselves with the Christian press would have pigeonholed their faith and their art.'

Steve Stockman, *Walk On: The Spiritual Journey of U2* (2001).

'Songwriting comes from a different place. Music is the language of the spirit. I think ideas and words are our excuses as songwriters to allow our heart or our spirit to run free. That's when magic happens.'

Bono, *Los Angeles Times* (August 2004).

'I got out before anybody else. I'd just had enough, it was bullshit. It was like joining the Moonies. So I left, then Bono left and then Edge left. And there was a period of time where Edge was really conflicted about whether the band could continue or not. There was a pretty robust conversation, and

Paul [McGuinness] was involved in it and so was Adam ... Paul's argument, in the end, is what kept the band going. I was happy enough to go on. Bono, I think, could have swung either way. We made the right decision.'

Larry Mullen Jr, on leaving the Christian organisation Shalom in the early 1980s, *Mojo* (July 2005).

'He had mischievousness in his eyes as well as godliness.'

Bono, on meeting Pope John Paul II on 23 September 1999, *Q* (May 2006).

'Coolness might help in your negotiation with people through the world, maybe, but it is impossible to meet God with sunglasses on. It is impossible to meet God without abandon, without exposing yourself, being raw.'

Bono on Bono (2005).

'He was the first blues singer.'

Bono, talking about the biblical figure of David, in John Waters, *Race of Angels – the Genesis of U2* (1994).

'Sadly, religion like politics attracts both the worst and the best kinds of people, often the worst.'

Bono, *Propaganda* (1987).

'I suppose it was the first time I was able to go, "Hang on, maybe these people are a little less stable than I thought!" Whereas up to that point I had always assumed that music and spirituality were on the same page – I didn't necessarily see it as a conflict. Having got a record out there, having toured it, they were prepared to go, "Actually, this isn't what we want." Whereas I, having tasted it, went, "Why wouldn't you? This is a more interesting and ultimately more satisfying journey than just staying in Dublin." So it was pretty baffling to me. And when I say baffling, I mean I really couldn't understand it.'

Adam Clayton, on the band's crisis of faith, *Mojo* (July 2005).

'I had the idea that no one can own Jerusalem, but everybody wants to put flags on it. The title's an ancient name that's not meant to be spoken. I got around it by singing. I hope I don't offend anyone.'

Bono, on the track 'Yahweh' on *How To Dismantle An Atomic Bomb*, *Q* (November 2004).

'Godliness is hard-wired into their system; angst'n'faith'n' rock'n'roll is what comes naturally. That it can work at all is a measure of pop's deepest paradox: that the endorphin-charged, chemically zapped rush you get in the eye of the big beat's reckless abandon is the closest most of us will get to the transcendent moments of epiphany spoken of by those touched by the divine. In short, God is in the guitar solo, and always has been. U2 instinctively know it...'

Mat Snow, writing in *Mojo* (March 1997).

'I've always believed that the spirit is a feminine thing.'

Bono, in Niall Stokes, *Into the Heart: The Stories behind Every U2 Song* (2001).

'[Adam] was extremely negative towards any religious organisation or anything spiritual. Adam thought this was dangerous and a real affront ... He came to me one day and said, "What are you doing? You're just doing this because of Bono. It's not you." I guess Adam's perception was that through force of personality, Bono was turning the group into a Christian group, and he was terrified of that idea. It upset him; he didn't get it.'

Edge, *U2 By U2* (October 2006).

'We have come to realise that [religion] is such a corruptible thing, that basically religion only works on an individual basis. That organised religion is so fragile and easily corrupted that you can't really trust it. I basically assume that every single group, or religious community, has a problem, is in some way screwed up. I don't believe that there is one single, perfect spiritual way and, in realising that, obviously you become a lot more open...'

Edge, *Hot Press* (October 1986).

'The music that really turns me on is either running towards God or away from God. Both recognise the pivot – that God is at the centre of the jaunt.'

Bono, *Rolling Stone* (3 November 2005).

'I wish to begin again on a daily basis. To be born again every day is something that I try to do. And I'm deadly serious about that.'

Bono on Bono (2005).

'If I had my say, a lot of the gospel tunes and hymns would be thrown out of the Vatican library. I think they're working much more for the devil ... They're saccharine sugar. It's such awful music, it must be an embarrassment to the Good

Lord. That's why I prefer the blues to gospel or punk rock to feelgood dance music. There's an honesty there, people owning up to their despair, and that's what religion should be more like, instead of this happy-clappy 'let's pretend we're not all afraid of dying'.'

Bono, *Q* (January 2006).

'I wish I could live the life of someone you could describe as pious. I couldn't preach because I couldn't practise. It's plain to see I'm not a good advertisement for God. Artists are selfish people.'

Bono on Bono (2005).

'The religious instinct is a very pure one in my opinion. But unless it's met with a lot of rigor it's very hard to control ... I don't let my religious world get too complicated. I just kind of go: well, I think I know what God is. God is love, and as much as I respond in allowing myself to be transformed by that love and acting in that love, that's my religion. Where things get complicated for me is when I try to live this love. Now, that's not so easy.'

Bono on Bono (2005).

'As a believer I want a bit of heaven on earth ... I'm not going to sign up for some religious organisation where I've got to accept wading in the sewers for seventy years on earth so we can all wear flowers in our hair when we die.'

Bono, *Vanity Fair* (November 2004).

'I have no trouble with Christ, but I have trouble with a lot of Christians. That was the problem. We wanted to give ourselves the chance to be viewed without that thing hanging over us. I don't think we're worried about it now. Also, at that stage we were going through our most out-there phase, spiritually. It was incredibly intense. We were just so involved with it. It was a time in our lives where we really concentrated on it more than on almost anything. Except Adam, who just wasn't interested.'

Edge, on the spiritual conflict U2 were experiencing at the time of their second album, *October*, in Bill Flanagan, *U2 at the End of the World* (1995).

'It sustains me.'

Bono, on the inspiration he received from the Bible, *Rolling Stone* (3 November 2005).

'Religious people, generally, they freak me out. Honestly, I start twitching when I'm around them. But sometimes, maybe weirdos are the only people who really know they need God.'

Bono on Bono (2005).

'I'm fascinated by anarchists ... The Judaeo/Christian belief in love as the higher law, the spirit leading you and no one knowing where it goes to – I think that's very close to anarchy.'

Bono, *Hot Press* (December 1988).

'No one wants to offend another's religious convictions. I have enormous respect for Islamic culture but I would encourage extremists to consider the murder of a novelist as sacrilegious to my faith. God does not need us as His bodyguard. Surely it's the other way around.'

Bono, on the issues surrounding the surprise appearance on stage of Salman Rushdie at Wembley Stadium on 11 August 1993, in *U2 By U2* (2006).

Politics

U2 have been making political statements for most of their career; it's a tricky thing being in a rock 'n' roll band (with all the associated trappings of the lifestyle) and having a conscience. Serious political pundits reckon that such a conscience is a tokenistic, hollow one. In particular, Bono has been accused, too many times to mention, of meddling in the affairs of nations when, really (they say) he should just stick to what he knows best – being a rock star. So it begs the questions: Where does conscience and duty start and where does conscience and duty end? Should rock stars facilely entertain? Or should they connect somehow with the serious issues of the day? U2 have refused to back away from engaging with political matters – from 'Sunday Bloody Sunday', 'Pride (In The Name Of Love)', the ZooTV link-ups to Sarajevo and the Vertigo tour's Guantanamo hostage stage play, the band have resolutely said what's on their minds, despite some critics saying that they don't know what they're on about. Our advice on the bottom line? Ask Larry.

'I think it's foolhardy. I think it's vain. I don't like it at any level. It's dangerous and uninsurable and seems to contradict something I thought we had all thought through. We came to the conclusion that the duty of the artist is to illustrate contradictions and point a finger at things that are wrong and terrible without the responsibility of having to resolve them. U2's efforts to discuss any humanitarian issue have sometimes been accompanied by a false instinct that U2 is also obliged to resolve that issue. Going to Sarajevo seems to me to fall into that category. I think it would endanger the people we go with, endanger the tour and endanger the band. I think it's grandstanding.'

Paul McGuinness, on Bono's determination to get ZooTV to Sarajevo, in Bill Flanagan, *U2 at the End of the World* (1995).

'The Bosnian link-up was beyond bad taste. It was insulting. Faced with the horrific description of the situation in Sarajevo, Bono was reduced to a stumbling incoherence that was probably the result of genuine concern, but came across as bog-standard celeb banality. What does the band who have virtually everything buy with their millions? The one thing they've never had – credibility. Shame it's not for sale.'

NME, on the ZooTV link-up to Sarajevo (August 1993).

'When it comes to discussing politics, I just want to be the man at the bar talking, that's all. No more or less educated about anything than anyone else.'

Bono, *Hot Press* (December 1988).

'It's true that there is a very painful aspect to it, because these people are living in a very stark life and death situation, and it felt very awkward ... One woman on the screen said, "You're not doing anything for us!" and the next stage is – you sing another song. That's very jagged. But it's exactly what I thought was valuable in it ... The awkwardness of it, the ill-fittingness, was what made it memorable. I've never been made, in a rock & roll show, to feel the pain of the world before. It's very easy to knock that stuff, and journalists by and large cultivate the kind of cynicism from which it becomes very easy to say it is done crassly. But I didn't feel that.'

Salman Rushdie, on the ZooTV link-up to Sarajevo, in Bill Flanagan, *U2 at the End of the World* (1995).

'It was unintentional. We met once on a plane, and in one election campaign he was good enough to allow me visit the studios and we took a few photographs, but anything beyond that ... I've a great respect for him personally, and for U2 and what they've done ... I went to one concert which I found extremely interesting ... but in that area I would not claim to be, er, up on it, or identify with it.'

Dr Garret FitzGerald, former Taoiseach, on his brief meeting with Bono in the early 1980s, *In Dublin* (24 October 1990).

'I'm available to be used, that is the deal here. I'll step out with anyone, but I'm not a cheap date. I know that I'm being used, and it's just at what price.'

Bono on Bono (2005).

'We rely on politicians too much. They don't necessarily have the skills to deal with a situation like this, or the vision.'

Edge, on the flooding in New Orleans, *The Independent* (16 May 2006).

'I've had enough of Irish Americans who haven't been back in their country for twenty or thirty years, who come up to me and talk about the resistance, the revolution back home, and the glory of the revolution and the glory of the dying for the revolution. Fuck the revolution! ... Where's the glory in taking a man from his bed and gunning him down in front of his wife and children? ... Where's the glory in bombing a Remembrance Day Parade of old-age pensioners – their medals taken out and polished up for the day? Where's the glory in that? To leave them dying or crippled for life or dead under the rubble of a revolution that the majority of the people in my country don't want. No more!'

Bono, speaking on stage at the McNichols Sports Arena, Denver, Colorado, on the same day that the IRA killed eleven people with a bomb in Enniskillen, County Fermanagh (8 November 1987).

'I think people understood where it came from, that there was a good reason. It was a reaction. It was taken not so much as political statement but as an emotional one which a lot of people shared, including some supporters of the Provisionals, I would have thought. Everyone would have felt that way.'

Bono, on the reaction to his speech at the McNichols Sports Arena, *Hot Press* (December 1988).

'We weren't worried that the IRA would start taking shots at a rock band.'

Paul McGuinness, *Q* (August 2006).

'After having denounced the IRA from a stage in Ireland in the early 1980s I remember a few incidents. Once, our car was surrounded by a bunch of Provo supporters. One had wrapped the Tricolor around his fist trying to smash the windows of the car with his bare hands, screaming, "Brits! Traitors!" However real or not, there was one threat of kidnapping, which the head of the Special Branch was taking very seriously. I remember we all had to have our toeprints taken as well as our fingerprints. That set the imagination off – were they gonna break our legs or post them?'

Bono on Bono (2005).

'I just let Bono get on with it. His judgement of these things has proved to be pretty good. He works very well in these arenas and understands the language. I don't necessarily feel qualified.'

Adam Clayton, on Bono's politicking, in *U2 By U2* (2006).

'I used to get ten or twenty applications a week for U2 to do some charity event or other. For every one they agreed to do, a few hundred would be rejected. The band had a very interesting view on these things. They wanted to be what they called 'the silver bullet', which meant that their participation would have to make a sizeable shift in the way that something would happen. They realised that if they went and did every political campaign or every charity, in the end it would just be like, "Oh, yeah. They're here again. So what?" They realised that their political capital had to be used carefully.'

Ian Flooks, agent, in Diana Scrimgeour, *U2 Show* (2004).

'So Governor Clinton doesn't think foreign policy is important, but anyway he's trying to catch up. You may have seen this in the news, he was in Hollywood, seeking foreign policy advice from the rock group U2. Now, understand, I have nothing against U2. You may not know this, but they're trying to call me at the White House every night during the concert. But the next time we face a foreign-policy crisis, I will work with John Major and Boris Yeltsin, and Bill Clinton can consult Boy George – I will stay with the experts.'

US President George Bush, as part of his speech on his presidential campaign (26 September 1992).

'I've met people the band would rather I didn't meet and there are some people I have to talk to, or appear in a photograph with, that in other circumstances I'd rather not.'

Bono, *Irish Independent* (28 July 2001).

'You always have some minor anxieties about such things. I think we felt that in all likelihood it probably would not change the already frosty mood that existed between us and the hardline Republicans. It was no news to them how we felt.'

Edge, *Q* (August 2006).

'If he wants to be taken seriously by the people that are fighting a war in Ireland and by the people who are dying left, right and centre, whether it's Loyalists or Republicans, he'll have serious conversations with them. He'd soon realise how utterly and totally and absolutely uninformed and ignorant he is. Take the time to go to Belfast or Derry and find out, or not even go there but meet up with people who are politically active in the war that goes on, from whatever side he cares to meet up with. He never chose to do that. He uses a major emotional tactic in order to look good.'

Fachtna O'Ceallaigh, former manager of The Boomtown Rats and Sinead O'Connor and one-time employee of U2's Mother Records, in Bill Flanagan, *U2 at the End of the World* (1995).

'They are a group for whom performance is always in some way political – no matter to what extent they package those politics in extravagant display. So back in 1979, by playing the outdoor shows especially for their younger fans, U2 were also making a statement about access and exclusivity: that inherent in pop and rock ... is the drive to give a voice and a face to the dispossessed.'

Michael Bracewell, in Diana Scrimgeour, *U2 Show* (2004).

'Czechoslovakia, East Germany, Poland, Romania ... all because of one man – The Edge.'

Bono, blaming U2's guitarist for political changes in Eastern Europe and the fall of the Iron Curtain, on stage at The Point, Dublin (26 December 1989).

'I wouldn't move to a smaller house.'

Bono, when asked if he wanted to be president of Ireland, in *Bono on Bono* (2005).

'Every decade needs a band that will stand up and reflect the spirit of its time without any shield. U2 did that in the 1980s and they are not going to do it any more, it's too painful.'

Bono, in Bill Flanagan, *U2 at the End of the World* (1995).

'When The Disposable Heroes of Hiphoprisy were on tour with U2, I was approached by a journalist who asked if I really thought that U2 were still a socially aware and political band. My answer was simple: every night for the past fifty nights I've seen 50,000 people come to a stadium and go home smiling. Now if you can tell me a politician who can do that, well I'll vote for 'em.'

Michael Franti, *Hot Press* (4 October 2006).

'U2 is about the impossible. Politics is the art of the possible. They're very different and I'm resigned to it now ... When you sing, you make people vulnerable to change in their lives. You make yourself vulnerable to change in your life. But in the end, you've got to become the change you want to see in the world.'

Bono, *Time* magazine (4 March 2002).

'If you give someone a colour television, a house, a car and two weeks vacation a year ... they'll agree to anything and stop asking questions.'

Bono, *Propaganda* (1987).

'If Bono ever decided to throw in the rock thing – which I very much doubt – he would have a huge future in Fianna Fáil.'

Bertie Ahern, Taoiseach, *Sunday Independent* (12 November 2006).

'Politicians are a little like priests and cops. They're either there for the best or the worst reasons: to serve or to abuse their power. But the latter are the few, not the many.'

Bono on Bono (2005).

'The position of any band talking about the topics of their day is always a very delicate one. The only justification I can give is that we are expressing our convictions. I can see how it can appear patronising, but it depends on one's motivations. There are a lot of things we could get pulled up on. If people don't like it, then that is understandable, but we will be standing by what we've done.'

Edge, *NME* (26 February 1983).

'When rock stars speak out on political issues I get nervous, and I am one. When musicians open their mouths to do anything but sing, I generally put my wallet in my boot, and yet music more than anything has kept my conscience. It's the noise that keeps me awake, stops me falling asleep in the comfort of this wild freedom some of us are enjoying on the eve of the twenty-first century.'

Bono, addressing the General Assembly of the United Nations, New York (September 1999).

'I admire him for doing it, but it creates serious, serious difficulties. He's running around trying to do everything and keep everybody happy. The reality is it's probably the most important thing he's going to do in his life, so my attitude would be to take a year out and do it properly.'

Larry Mullen Jr, on Bono's political activism, Q (July 2001).

'I don't have any real power, but the people I represent do. The reason why politicians let me in the door, and the reason why people take my call is because I represent quite a large constituency of people ... I represent them in a certain sense, even without them asking me to, in the minds of the people whose doors I knock upon.'

Bono on Bono (2005).

'Some people I've met have made me sick to the stomach. I can't tell you their names because I still have to work with them. But I've also got to like a lot of very conservative people. I find their up-frontness can be more refreshing than my liberal friends, who tell me everything's possible but sometimes don't want to follow through.'

Bono, Q (November 2004).

'It's something that we've been criticised for. That's such a complex issue that to get politically involved is actually not right. However, Bono has always stood up, has been quoted on several occasions, saying violence is not the way. We've always said violence is not the answer, it's not going to solve anything. And Bono's reaction that was put in *Rattle And Hum* ("Fuck the revolution!") was the biggest political statement you could make! There's no chance we're going to get involved in party politics. That is not what we are. We're not good at that. We are able to stand up and make a social statement that killing people is not the way to solve anything, be that the IRA, the PLO or whoever it is. We've never been silent on those issues.'

Larry Mullen Jr, on being asked whether U2 deliberately avoided making statements about the Irish political situation, in Bill Flanagan, *U2 at the End of the World* (1995).

'Everybody wants to live in America. Not me. I love this city. I hate what some of those bastards have done to it: boring, unimaginative politicians, the arrogant architects, the back-handed builders. Let them go to fuckin' America.'

Bono, on stage at The Point, Dublin (27 December 1989).

'I fancy Mrs Thatcher but I think she's gonna have to go.'

Bono, on stage at Wembley Arena, London (2 June 1987).

'We've grown up being a political band. We never saw a need to separate religion and politics from everything we write about and care about. We have always been well aware that steaming in on any issue was liable to get us into trouble, or just come off as uncool. My own real fear was that Bono was going to lead us into doing things that were desperately uncool ... But even though I have winced on his behalf, I've had more times when I've just been so proud of him and blown away with the success of what he's done.'

Edge, *Sunday Times Magazine* (7 November 2004).

'It doesn't necessarily help our band that Bono is so well known now as a political activist. It's great on one level, but being photographed with George W. Bush and the Pope – I don't like it particularly and he knows it ... At the end of the day, I had to agree that if you can help hundreds of thousands, maybe millions of people's lives ... I just worry that with political work it's a murky business. You never really know if the deal you're getting is the deal you think you're getting. He's had to make certain compromises I'm not sure I would be comfortable making.'

Edge, *Vanity Fair* (November 2004).

'My soul would shrivel if I had to be a politician full-time. I need to make music with my brothers.'

Bono, *Q* (January 2006).

'Most of our audience probably don't see us as a political band, but an aware band – which is what we really are.'

Adam Clayton, speaking in a syndicated US radio interview (December 1984).

'You can't but be in awe of the strength of will that it took for Bobby Sands to go on that hunger strike, but I just don't know – there are people striving to hold on to life. There are people in other countries who are dying because they have no food, not because they are refusing food. To me, their reality is something that we must not forget about. I don't deny that some of the wishes of the IRA and some of the people who support the Provisional IRA are sincere, but they are, in my opinion, sincerely wrong.'

Bono, *Hot Press* (December 1988).

'If people want to use our songs, we have a policy of turning a blind eye. Especially if it's somebody you admire, and I admire Tony Blair.'

Bono, *Mojo* (July 2005).

'It's no fun being seen as a political group if you don't know that much about politics, but I know a little about people ... You've got to find your place and my place is doing what I'm best at, which is making music. That's the best way I can challenge a system or inspire people. I've never pointed a finger at anyone other than myself in my songs. We don't write songs about 'you' or 'they', it's always about 'we' or 'I' with U2.'

Bono, speaking in a radio interview on Boston's WBCN (December 1984).

'You've got to start with your own hypocrisy before you start pointing it out in politicians.'

Bono, *Time Out* (25 November 1992).

'It was a struggle to get the balance right.'

Larry Mullen Jr, on Bono's speechifying during the Vertigo tour, in *U2 By U2* (2006).

'After some initial doubts, the band came around. I mean, Larry would be looking at his watch whenever I started speaking at the opening of 'One'. He forgets he's on camera at all times, and people are watching him as he's watching his watch. He's timing me to see how long the speech would go on ... Priceless. In Washington DC, when we had all the politicians there, I went on for fifteen minutes. Larry was nodding off behind me, in full view of various congressmen and women.'

Bono, on his speechifying during the Vertigo tour, in *U2 By U2* (2006).

Bush, Clinton and America

It's a cliché for any successful rock band to say that they have a special relationship with America, but in U2's case it happens to be true. It's true because from the early 1980s, they assiduously spent more time touring around the United States than probably (this is an unscientific assumption) any other band of their current status. Small venues in places such as Boise, Idaho, were grist to the U2 mill during the first half of that decade. From then on, however, it all got a bit fuzzy – *The Joshua Tree* and *Rattle And Hum* albums and tours saw the band treat the US as a creative touchstone. In the end, it gave them a nasty love bite, which is surely one of the reasons why they subsequently retreated to Berlin to record *Achtung Baby* and enter into a new phase of evangelical irony versus preacher-man earnestness.

'After 9/11, our audience was very porous, very vulnerable, very open. They really didn't know what was going to happen next. It's worth remembering, those of us who came out against the war, that in the United States they really thought it was a matter of weeks or months till the next hit happened, and what's it going to be – some suitcase bomb taking out a corner of Chicago? They were on tenterhooks. The fists were up but they were very vulnerable.'

Bono, *Music Express*, on Ireland's RTÉ2 (June 2005).

'The Superbowl was a big moment for U2, almost like our *Ed Sullivan Show*, twenty years on. We had to build that stage in six minutes. I was on radio-controlled earphones and microphone. One error and you're off air. It was terrifying, but all you can see is my usual expression when I'm terrified – a big smirk. But it was a great moment. That whole tour, we kind of fell in love with America again and they fell in love with us.'

Bono, in *U2 By U2* (2006).

'I find it hard to believe she would pass up an opportunity to lobby the president on behalf of Operation Smile. It's never been a problem for Bono.'

Carl Forti, US National Republican Congressional Committee spokesman, on singer/actress Jessica Simpson turning down an invitation to meet US President George W. Bush for a fundraiser, *Ireland on Sunday* (March 2006).

'It's a very, very strange place, that's why I'm into it, cos it's so fucking weird. There's no heart to that city. I've been there ten times, but it was only on this trip that I actually found Hollywood!'

Edge, on Hollywood, *Hot Press* (October 1988).

'[George Bush] banged the table at me once, when I was ranting at him about the ARVs (AIDS drugs) not getting out quick enough ... He banged the table to ask me to let him reply. He smilingly reminded me he was the president. It was a heated debate. I was very impressed he could get so passionate and, let's face it, tolerating an Irish rock star is not a necessity of his office.'

Bono on Bono (2005).

'I have a kind of love-hate relationship with America. I love the place, I love the people. One of the things I hate is that such a trusting place could have put their trust in a guy like Ronald Reagan. He may be a sincere man, but he is sincerely wrong in so many cases.'

Bono, *Propaganda* (1987).

'We wanted to be in the US. It was where we belonged ... U2 have always had a special relationship with New York. It was the first city we played in America. There was the Irish connection, there was the magic of the city itself. Myself and Adam have had apartments in New York for over ten years. Bono recently got a place there. We have always seen it as a second home.'

Larry Mullen Jr, on 9/11, in *U2 By U2* (2006).

'For the Irish, the concept of moving away to another country and working hard and doing well there is a very big part of Irish history. And we saw America as just another place to go and work and do some shows and try and sell a few albums. We really didn't see it in any different light from Britain. We just got on with it. There was some big stigma for the English groups about being big in America, which is bollocks. Why should there be?'

Edge, *Q* (January 1993).

'You really have to look in this country to find out what's happening. When we first came here, America was like walking into an episode of *Starsky & Hutch*. Everybody would talk the same ... But once we were here two or three times, we were able to refine. We were like prospectors, coming here to find the gold. It wasn't easy.'

Edge, *Hot Press* (December 1987).

'In many ways, the Americans are innocent and more honest than us. They're very wide-eyed, it seems, but they make up their minds by instinct and I think that's very healthy. The reason that music is stale over here is that they haven't been given a chance to let their instinct go to work. But when it does, it sparks.'

Bono, *Hot Press* (1 May 1981).

'U2 never saw America as their antagonist ... From 1977 on, most new English bands outside the heavy-metal camp would distance themselves from those earlier exemplars. In contrast, U2 would pick up those classic role models without ever feeling guiltily out of sync.'

Bill Graham, *Hot Press* (December 1989).

'You know the bit in the show where I put a headband on over my eyes, I take on this kind of hostage thing and then we put on the declaration of human rights? People are clapping nervously, because they don't know if we're getting at them ... So there's been an uneasiness in America about that part of the show – "Are they getting at us?" – and then we say, "No, we're just making a point."'

Bono, *Music Express*, on Ireland's RTÉ2 (June 2005).

'A great leader has to have a great ear for melody. By this, I mean clarity of ideas. What I think they might all have in common, the ones I've met – if they're any good – is an ability to see through the din and clangour of ideas and conversations and points of view, and hear the melody line, and realise: this is the thing we've got to do; this is more important than the others. They're like talent scouts in the music business, A&R men for ideas. Bill Clinton was incredible at spotting an idea.'

Bono on Bono (2005).

'I have to apply for a visa six weeks in advance of travelling and it makes it hard to be spontaneous. Even when you do get a visa, when you arrive you get sent to a little back room where they basically humiliate you, then eventually look in your passport, stamp it and let you go. I just wonder if it happens to Paul McCartney?! Maybe not. Maybe being busted with a bag of grass in Japan is a different offence.'

Adam Clayton, on his 'issues' with the US immigration authorities, *Mojo* (July 2005).

'I just can't get over New York. It feels like the centre of the earth. Which is, I'm sure, why Osama Bin Laden singled it out. It's certainly the city of our times, as Paris and London have been in the past, the centre of Western culture. I have an apartment there, and I'm lucky to be able to live in it, walk around in it and experience the intense heat of New York summers. There have been times in my life when I have gotten lost there ... and it is a great city to get lost in.'

Bono, in *U2 By U2* (2006).

Africa

Anyone who doubts Bono's sense of goodwill towards the poor and starving in Africa is a fool. And anyone who sneers at his attempts to help such a situation requires psychiatric attention. Beyond anyone operating out of the 'entertainment' industry (bar Bob Geldof, who these days is known more as a shrewd entrepreneur than as a musician), Bono has made it his business to learn about global strategies on and about the Third World. Whether he's addressing a special session on Africa's future at the World Economic Forum or whether he's speaking on the topic in his capacity as founder of DATA (Debt, Aid and Trade for Africa), he seems so in charge of his subject it's no wonder he has gained the respect of people who, ten years previously, might have looked at him with disdain.

'Bono has done incredible work with the debt cancellation and the AIDS problem in Africa, but we wince sometimes when we see him with politicians in the newspaper. It's worth it, but sometimes you realise how some people are going, "Wanker!"'

Edge, *Q* (November 2002).

'We've all asked him if this is something he can defend, and he's said, "I've been to Africa, I've seen people dying from starvation. I've been to AIDS hospitals and seen people dying from AIDS. If I have to have lunch with the devil himself to get people to help and do something, I'll do it." You can't really counter that.'

Larry Mullen Jr, *Vanity Fair* (November 2004).

'I feel that the arc of my own life as an activist is not unlike that of a lot of other people: we started off responding to a need, then started to be informed about what had caused that need, and then went on to discover that the response to the need was not exactly what we originally thought it was.'

Bono, on his campaigning for Africa, *The Irish Times* (2006).

'Bono and Bob Geldof have been useful idiots for Bush and Blair on the whole G8 affair and on other issues. I heard Bono say that Bush has made a remarkable impact on Africa. Please. I think they're both [Bono/Geldof] an example of the saying that a little knowledge is dangerous ... They can't make the policy for the campaign because they don't know enough and therefore people can run rings around them.'

George Galloway MP, *Q* (June 2006).

'I have watched these brave and beautiful souls who are fighting a forest fire of a pandemic with watering cans, knowing they will not see the light of day when their work will be honoured. I have been witness to their conversations around canteen tables, deciding who will live or die, because they do not have enough pills to go around ... And so I testify.'

Bono, *The Independent* (16 May 2006).

'We wanted to make the fight against AIDS in Africa sexy and smart. We needed to create heat in areas where we haven't had a presence, such as the high street.'

Bono, on (RED), the customised products from companies such as Gap, Armani, Converse and American Express, *Happy* (April 2006).

'I first went to Africa, to Ethiopia, to work in a feeding station following Live Aid in 1985 – one summer that stayed with me for a lifetime ... But I don't see Africa as a cause. To me, this whole thing is about justice. The fact that 6,300 people die in Africa every day of AIDS, a preventable, treatable disease, for lack of drugs that we take for granted in Europe and America – that's about justice, not charity.'

Bono, World Association of Newspapers (May 2004).

'When it comes to the time to write the history of this, it will be their names that will be important. Not mine.'

Bono, speaking about African women on anti-retroviral drugs for their HIV condition, *The Observer* (21 May 2006).

'I'm not sure if it's Catholic guilt or what, but I genuinely believe that second only to personal redemption, the most important thing in the Scriptures – 2,103 passages in all – refers to taking care of the world's poor.'

Bono, *Los Angeles Times* (April 2005).

'If we really thought that an African life was equal in value to an English, a French or an Irish life, we wouldn't let two and a half million Africans die every year for the stupidest of reasons: money. We just wouldn't. And a very prominent head of state said to me: "It's true. If these people weren't Africans, we just couldn't let it happen." We don't really deep down believe in their quality.'

Bono on Bono (2005).

'I got more than I gave to Ethiopia. My head was in the clouds and my feet were not on the ground.'

Bono, on his visit to Ethiopa in 1985, *Q* (August 2006).

'I don't want to be doing this other job is the truth ... It's an accident of fate that I ended up in this place. I think I'm much better being in a band.'

Bono, on running with the politicians, *Larry King Live* show (December 2002).

'At periods in your life, you start to doubt yourself. A third of the world is starving to death and you're in a rock 'n' roll group getting completely overpaid for doing a job that you would do for nothing.'

Bono, *Vanity Fair* (November 2004).

'One of the hardest things that happened to me in my entire life happened in the mid-1980s ... It was a man, this beautiful, noble African man, handing me his child, and saying "Please, take this child. Because if you take it, the child will live and be educated, and if you don't he will surely die." And I didn't take the child. So I'm very happy that Madonna bought a first-class ticket for a poor African. I think that's amazing.'

Bono, on being asked what his stance was on Madonna adopting an African baby, *Q* (January 2007).

Albums

U2 were once thought of as an albums band – a throwback to the days of prog rock when it was thought that having hit singles was the preserve of pop groups. Hit singles = pop = frivolous; hit albums = rock = significant. It's all changed now, of course, and U2 are successful in each area, but U2 albums are still recognised as 'event' occasions: people queue up outside record stores days before an album is released in the hope that they'll be among the first to get their hands on the brand new record. U2, also, take the release of a record seriously; certainly, they're not the most prolific of rock acts, which means that each album is viewed (as much by their fans as by music critics, not that the two are indivisible) as a genuine artefact of shared, committed creative conception and birth. With a great deal of frustration thrown in.

'I would like to do that album again, if nothing else to stop singing like Siouxsie Sioux, who I was listening to a lot at that time. And I wasn't even thinking about lyrics – they're just sketches. I'm definitely the person who let that album down.

It's one of the best debut albums ever. And if I'd sung in my own accent and finished the lyrics, it might have been really good.'

Bono, on *Boy*, *Mojo* (July 2005).

'It is really the most expensive demo session in the history of music.'

Bono, on *Pop*, in *U2 By U2* (2006).

'They'd go and fly off to wherever they were in Europe, do their gig and fly back. We worked according to their instructions during the day. They'd usually get back anytime between 11 p.m. and 1 a.m. Then they'd come in, have a listen, make more comments. I can remember doing vocals with Bono for 'Lemon' at 4 a.m. Insane, insane hours. It nearly killed all of us. We were constantly in this state of stressed caffeine hallucinations, hiding in the studio. It was ridiculous.'

Flood, record producer, on the making of *Zooropa*, in Diana Scrimgeour, *U2 Show* (2004).

'U2's records take a long time to make not because the band members are stuck for ideas but because they never stop talking about them.'

Brian Eno, *Rolling Stone* (28 November 1991).

'The Edge Orchestra.'

Bill Graham, giving a definition of U2's sound on *War*, *Hot Press* (March 1983).

'It was a bloody difficult album to make but a lot less difficult than the alternative. If we hadn't done something we were excited about, that made us apprehensive and challenged everything we stood for, then there would really have been no reason to carry on. We were at a watershed. If it hadn't been a great record by our standards, the existence of the band would have been threatened.'

Adam Clayton, on *Achtung Baby*, in *U2 By U2* (2006).

'If I was able to predict what their next album would look or sound like, well then we've failed because there should always be an element of surprise.'

Steve Averill, designer, *The Irish Times Magazine* (25 August 2001).

'I have to say there's a side of me that can't quite work out why anyone would buy a U2 LP. I think I might buy one...'

Bono, *Propaganda* (1987).

'U2 work very hard, they're perfectionists, but work expands to fill the time available to do it. I still find it amazing they can concentrate for such a long time on a record and I'm bemused that they don't write the songs before they record them. Chris Thomas [co-producer] came to see me one day and said, "I've never worked with any artist where nothing is prepared, nothing is demoed, they just go in and wait for it to arrive. I feel I'm letting them down." I said, "This is the way it always is and actually it's going rather well."'

Paul McGuinness, on the recording of *How To Dismantle An Atomic Bomb*, in *U2 By U2* (2006).

'It is a fight. It's us versus The Obvious Route For U2 Right Now, which would be mediocrity, cult sales and living off your past. And it's a grudge match, it really is. We're going into this like it's our first album. And that's what makes it taut, tight and economic. This record is verse-chorus-and-here's-another-chorus-just-in-case-you-missed-the-last-one. And it's like – follow that.'

Bono, on *All That You Can't Leave Behind*, Q (November 2000).

'It dawned on us after *The Joshua Tree* that the bigness of U2 had become a distraction. I remember thinking that we were in a position where we really didn't have to do anything any more ... The only thing we could do was split up or pour all our confusion into the music. In some ways, *Achtung Baby* is the sound of a band fighting for its musical life. To me, it's like a first album, the beginning of U2 Mark 2.'

Larry Mullen Jr, *The Face* (April 1992).

'It was a train off the tracks. We were going to premieres all around the world and it was being billed as 'The Great Rock 'N' Roll Movie'. It was enough to make a lot of people throw up. And y'know what? It made me throw up, too. I really regret it. I think as a road movie, whether you like U2 or not, you would have gone and thought it was really special. But it was all lights, action, Hollywood. We fucked up.'

Larry Mullen, on *Rattle And Hum* – the movie, *Mojo* (July 2005).

'We're on a roll. It's getting more like the early U2 records. Really simple, stripped-down arrangements. That's what we're hungry for – music with that life force.'

Edge, on *How To Dismantle An Atomic Bomb*, Q (November 2002).

'*Achtung Baby* and *Zooropa* were masterpieces. This whole period was like a vortex fraught with danger because there were so many different avenues being explored, a serious amount of sonic frontier was being breached, crossed and extended. Dan Lanois with Brian Eno and Flood established directives and areas to experiment. Bono would basically keep changing things around and turn everything on its head. He would drive everybody nuts, but inevitably get the best possible results.'

Joe O'Herlihy, U2 audio director, in Diana Scrimgeour, *U2 Show* (2004).

'This is just the end of something for U2, and that's why we're playing these concerts. We're throwing a party for ourselves and for you. It's no big deal, we have to go away and just dream it all up again.'

Bono, paving the way for *Achtung Baby* and the next phase of U2, at The Point, Dublin (27 December 1989).

'I don't think we're bright enough to be that calculating ... You can only get to ... *Atomic Bomb* after you've done *Pop*. You only get there because of that. And that's what interesting about the journey.'

Larry Mullen Jr, responding to the theory that *All That You Can't Leave Behind* and *How To Dismantle An Atomic Bomb* were made specifically to counteract the creative failure of *Pop*, *Mojo* (July 2005).

'The themes [on *Pop*] are love, desire and faith in crisis – the usual stuff.'

Edge, *Q* (March 1997).

'I was the one really pushing for the change in direction, and Edge was the one most supportive. There were times when Adam and Larry were actually antagonistic. But again, for reasons of modesty, they felt our reach couldn't meet our grasp.'

Bono, on the creative changes of *Achtung Baby*, in *Bono on Bono* (2005).

'Buzzwords on this record were trashy, throwaway, dark, sexy and industrial (all good) and earnest, polite, sweet, righteous, rockist and linear (all bad). It was good if a song took you on a journey or made you think that your hi-fi was broken, bad if it reminded you of recording studios or U2.'

Brian Eno, on the creative thrust behind *Achtung Baby*, *Rolling Stone* (28 November 1991).

'We realised that there's only a certain amount of Joshua Trees you can chop down.'

Larry Mullen Jr, on *All That You Can't Leave Behind*, *Q* (November 2002).

'I went into that record looking good. Then one day they had a guy doing hair in the studio. Bono said, "Dan, why don't you get a haircut?" I came out with a fucking mullet! I'll never forgive them.'

Daniel Lanois, co-producer on *The Joshua Tree*, *Q* (August 2006).

'Our goal is to write the perfect album. Every time we go into the studio, we hope we'll get closer to that. But I very much doubt we'll ever attain that goal of perfection. It's like Mount Everest. That must be a terribly depressing place; you've spent all your time preparing to get up there, and when you get there all you can do is walk down again.'

Edge, *Vanity Fair* (November 2004).

'We want to make a record that pushes out the boundaries a bit, not just for ourselves but in terms of what people are used to hearing on the radio or on records. We want to start abusing the technology that's available ...'

Bono, on the aspirations behind the making of *Achtung Baby*, *Propaganda* (1991).

'It was like, oh my God, this record isn't very good. But that was because of the time constraints. If we'd had an extra month, we'd have been able to do a lot more with some of the songs.'

Larry Mullen Jr, on *Pop*, *Q* (November 2002).

'*Pop* is an album which begins with the throb of the disco, and finishes in the silence of God. In between, they've looked for Him in the strangest places. And frankly, they sound shagged out by the effort.'

Review of *Pop*, *Q* (April 1997).

'We wanted to make a party record but we came in at the end of the party. The dancing was over and there were a load of broken bottles and young people sleeping under tables and the odd row in the garden between lovers who've imbibed too much.'

Bono, on *Pop*, in *U2 By U2* (2006).

'There's a thin line between making interesting music and being self-indulgent. We crossed that several times on

Passengers. In U2, we have opposing opinions on *Passengers*. Mine is that it's a lot of very, very bad self-indulgent music ... Not that the drums were ever self-indulgent, but all that other shit ...'

Larry Mullen Jr, *Q* (March 1997).

'It's the sound of a rock band finding its social conscience and trying to change the world, made at a time when the world still believed a rock band could make a difference.'

The Joshua Tree tops the charts of *Q* magazine's Best Records of the 1980s poll (August 2006).

'It's very hard sometimes to work on something for a long period of time, prepare for it, present it to the band, and then receive deafening silence, or the sound of a jaw opening and a yawn coming out. But Adam and Larry have very high standards and, usually, if it's really great, they will be very interested. But even then, they won't be hugely excited.'

Bono on Bono (2005).

'I remember having to do interviews and being asked what the album was about, and I had no ... fucking ... idea.'

Larry Mullen Jr, on *Pop*, *Q* (November 2000).

'I'm not comfortable with any one particular genre of music. I just like the idea of taking whatever's out there and fucking with it. It's very easy to just lose what's special about a band through technology, and we've touched on that a couple of times. *Zooropa* was the start of it and we got away with it, but in *Passengers* we were just about to cross over into an area that I wasn't comfortable with.'

Larry Mullen Jr, *Q* (March 1997).

'For all its naïveté and for all its stained-glass approach to lyric writing, if Joy Division were mining the gothic end of a very large cathedral, *October* was the folk mass/rave...'

Bono, *Mojo* (July 2005).

'The best thing about *The Joshua Tree* – marvellous and magnificent as it is – is that they can do ten times better.'

Paul McGuinness, *Propaganda* (1987).

'It started out to be a rock 'n' roll album, pure and simple. We were very excited that Edge wasn't sitting at the piano or twiddling a piece of technology ... Halfway through, we got bored, because it turns out you can only go so far with rifferama. We wanted more dimension. Now you've got punk rock starting points that go through Phil Spectorland, turn right at Tim Buckley, end up in alleyways and open onto other vistas and cityscapes and rooftops and skies. It's songwriting by accident, by a punk band that wants to play Bach.'

Bono, on *How To Dismantle An Atomic Bomb*.

'I thought they were very smart. Smart enough to look outside of themselves to get some inspiration. You have to admire somebody for being that humble, even though you're at the top of your game, to be humble enough to accept outside input.'

Daniel Lanois, co-producer on *The Unforgettable Fire*, *Mojo* (July 2005).

'The significant thing about [*The Joshua Tree*] is that I had to 'come clean' as a word-writer. Instead of trying to capture the elusive message of the music, which is what I'd normally try to do with my words, I wanted to speak out specifically, but without a placard, and without my John Lennon handbook.'

Bono, *Propaganda* (1987).

''The Fly' [lead single from *Achtung Baby*], well to me it's the sound of four men chopping down *The Joshua Tree*.'

Bono, *Propaganda* (1991).

'It's very difficult to pin this record down. It's not got an identity because it's got so many.'

Edge, on *Pop, Propaganda* (1997).

'The first thing I started writing about was death ... *Boy*, our first album, is remarkably uplifting, considering the subject matter. Oddly enough, it's similar to *How To Dismantle An Atomic Bomb*. It's something to do with the end of innocence, but [with *Boy*] it was being savoured, not remembered.'

Bono on Bono (2005).

'There's a bit of a sense of loss when you finish a record. For a long time you have a purpose every day, going in there and working on it. It's an intense, intimate environment.'

Adam Clayton, *Q* (March 1997).

'Love and sex, in and out of harmony – that's one vein that runs through the whole album. The idea of love that you keep on hearing about in songs – love is all you need, love is the drug – what does it mean anymore? When you actually see love go wrong, that's when you see its ugliness.'

Bono, on *Achtung Baby, The Face* (April 1992).

'We wanted to recognise ourselves more ... Wanted to own up to our ambitions, wanted to own up to our sexuality, wanted to own up to our own hypocrisy. So the hypocrisy of the human heart became the subject of this series of songs, which is really one song: it's a lovers' row. On *Achtung Baby*, it didn't look like it was gonna get patched up at all.'

Bono, on *Achtung Baby*, *Mojo* (July 2005).

'If we went down in flames on this one then I'd die happy.'

Larry Mullen Jr, on *All That You Can't Leave Behind*, *Q* (November 2000).

'*Achtung Baby.*'

Winner of the 50 Worst Album Titles of All Time, *Q* (February 1998). Runner-up titles included *From the Tearooms of Mars to the Hellholes of Uranus* (Landscape) and *A Salt With A Deadly Pepa* (Salt-N-Pepa).

'At one point we were going to call it *Pop – For Men. Pop Pour Hommes*. See, this is the record where the group really have the hips.'

Bono, *Q* (March 1997).

'It was a mistake, but maybe it had to be made.'

Larry Mullen Jr, on *Rattle And Hum*, *The Face* (April 1992).

'I think it was a glorious failure.'

Bono, on *Rattle And Hum*, *The Face* (April 1992).

'It's the most sonically inventive U2 record.'

Daniel Lanois, co-producer on *Achtung Baby*, *Mojo* (July 2005).

'It looks great on T-shirts.'

Larry Mullen Jr, on why the *Pop* album was so titled, *Mojo* (March 1997).

'*Achtung Baby* is definitely a reaction to the myth of U2. We never really had any control over that myth. You could say we helped it along a bit, but the actual myth itself is a creation of the media and people's imagination. There is little resemblance to the actual personalities of the band or the intentions of the band.'

Edge, *Musician* (March 1992).

'There was some dark stuff going around. I'd be lying to you if I said that there was no appeal to me in the, y'know, the abyss. Everyone wants to slip out of daylight and into the shadows. It's a more comfortable place to be sometimes ... I just can't fully surrender to the party. I just can't quite do it ... The love and lust for life on that record is very real.'

Bono, on *All That You Can't Leave Behind*, *Q* (July 2001).

'With *The Joshua Tree* and *Rattle And Hum*, it all became so big and such a blur that we lost touch with what was good about the band. The music suffered.'

Larry Mullen Jr, *Q* (January 1993).

'I'm not as emotionally attached to it as I am to *All That You Can't Leave Behind*. It just doesn't quite hang together as well as that album. It may be to do with the mix of personalities involved but it seems to be missing that same emotional thread.'

Larry Mullen Jr, on *How To Dismantle An Atomic Bomb*, in *U2 By U2* (2006).

'Bono was emotionally attached to the title. In the end, his instincts were correct.'

Larry Mullen Jr, on *How To Dismantle An Atomic Bomb*, in *U2 By U2* (2006).

'*Zooropa* is the sound of U2 becoming comfortable with a new recording environment. After the attrition of *Achtung Baby*, it was clear that this technology stuff was OK, it's not the Devil, it's not the enemy, we can work with it. Edge was still exploring dance and hip-hop culture, club mixes, all that kind of thing. He was experimenting and U2 were his guinea pigs.'

Larry Mullen Jr, in *U2 By U2* (2006).

'I think it's our best album, although perhaps not our most innovative. We may have succeeded almost too much in making an album showcasing the band because I think some of the songs could have gone into a more experimental area sonically. But as a collection of songs, it's our best ever.'

Edge, on *How To Dismantle An Atomic Bomb*, in *U2 By U2* (2006).

'It's wonderful, probably their greatest. Bono sings better than he has sung for years and so often in the work of the band the fact that his voice is the lead instrument gets forgotten ... I wasn't so excited about the title. Indeed, I'm still not crazy about it. There was quite a bit of discussion about that. But it is a creative matter and though I will air my views, I don't expect [them] to prevail.'

Paul McGuinness, on *How To Dismantle An Atomic Bomb*, in *U2 By U2* (2006).

'It was very hard work and expectations were high, as usual, in the U2 camp, and I think we really did it. It's ground breaking, it's fantastically out of control. It's wild, you don't know where it's coming from, it's bizarre and it's rock and roll. I love it.'

Daniel Lanois, record producer, on *Achtung Baby*, in Diana Scrimgeour, *U2 Show* (2004).

'I never thought of *Zooropa* as anything more than an interlude ... but a great one, as interludes go. By far our most interesting.'

Edge, in *U2 By U2* (2006).

Album Covers

Blame the lack of nous about style, image and fashion in the early part of their career for some of the most visually bland (if very well designed) album covers in rock. While the covers of *Boy* and *War* have down through the years justifiably achieved iconic status, it wasn't until Anton Corbijn's cover shot for *The Joshua Tree* that people twigged the band could actually look at you in a certain way and not come across as shelf stackers from Dunnes Stores or Wal Mart. It all went design-loopy for the 'European' trilogy of *Achtung Baby*, *Zooropa* and *Pop*, and then settled back into straight lines for the remainder. Truthfully, though, you would have thought that one of the most successful rock bands in the world might have wanted to lead the way in album cover visuals as their stage shows have done. It's a funny old world, etc.

'We hadn't a clue how to be art-directed or stylised for something like that. It was just very naïve, put the four lads together and shoot the photograph ... A lot of people tried to dissuade us; representatives from Island Records came over and told us, "The cover stinks." But we were so much up our own arses that we didn't have the sense to listen to what was being said.'

Adam Clayton, on the cover of *October*, in *U2 By U2* (2006).

'We sent him back to London and told them it was in the contract that we could have the sleeve we wanted. I have to say, he was absolutely right and we would have been much better off listening to him.'

Edge, on the cover of *October*, in *U2 By U2* (2006).

'We've always controlled our own graphics and packaging and timing, and, for a long time, we thought that every group did that.'

Paul McGuinness, *Propaganda* (1987).

'One of the few stadium bands not to have succumbed to the disco-remix, U2 are the Led Zeppelin of the consumer decade, The Dark Side of the Joshua Tree their most cohesive product to date – the revenge of the gatefold sleeve.'

The Face (September 1988).

'The look the band was going for was a displaced European immigrant arriving in the desert.'

Adam Clayton, on the cover shot of *The Joshua Tree*, in *U2 By U2* (2006).

'The cover is aesthetically low key, with none of that kind of Mount Rushmore iconography some people associate with U2 ... It's an ode to an airport. And it fits with the title perfectly. What's the destination? The future. And then, just because advertising pays, I thought I'd put God's phone number up in the airport's digital clock. J33:3. That's Jeremiah 33:3. The Scripture is: "Call unto Me and I will answer you." It's celestial telephony.'

Bono, on the cover of *All That You Can't Leave Behind*, in *U2 By U2* (2006).

'[The cover of *Boy*] became almost iconic, associated with that sense of innocence they had as a band. For every album cover we've done together since, there's been a large amount of discussion about how things work and what they do – it was a very strong path we were following. You've always got to be able to come up with something they like, that they find exciting, that they find is suitable for the music. You can't become complacent about doing it. You've got to be on your toes; graphically and musically you've got to match what they're doing.'

Steve Averill, designer of all U2 record and tour artwork, in Diana Scrimgeour, *U2 Show* (2004).

Music

Well, here's a tussle. Inevitably, it's all in the ear of the beholder, but we'll warrant that if you've bought this rather fine book then you're more than likely a fan of U2's music (unless you're a journalist who got the book for free, but we'll take our chances). Some people are of the opinion that until 'Pride (In The Name Of Love)' came along, U2 didn't have a songwriting sensibility. Others reckon that from 'Out Of Control' onwards, U2 have been throwing out great songs left, right and centre. Unquestionably, there seems to be an attitude of wanting to get the music 100 per cent right, but as anyone knows there's a significant difference between wanting and achieving. When they get it absolutely right ('Running To Stand Still'/*The Joshua Tree*; 'Who's Gonna Ride Your Wild Horses'/*Achtung Baby*; 'Kite'/*All That You Can't Leave Behind*; 'Sometimes You Can't Make It On Your Own'/*How To Dismantle An Atomic Bomb*) there's no one to beat them. When they get it wrong (a few off *October*; a few off *War*; most of *Pop*; several off *How To Dismantle An Atomic Bomb*), U2 come across as also-rans on a very big budget.

'U2 are the world's worst wedding band ... Why don't we just own up to it and stop fucking about? For instance, we were always jealous of the fact that we never knew anyone else's songs. That started a lot of B-sides where we started to do cover versions and tried to get into the structure of songwriting vicariously and then apply it. This is a band that's one of the biggest acts in the world, and we know fuck-all in terms of what most musicians would consider to be important.'

Bono, in Bill Flanagan, *U2 at the End of the World* (1995).

'I could tell they were dreamers ... optimists who just want to know what's on the other side of the hill.'

Daniel Lanois, record producer, in Diana Scrimgeour, *U2 Show* (2004).

'The test of a good song is that you should be able to sit down with an acoustic guitar and sing it. And it should still retain its power. I wouldn't have said that U2 would have passed that test in the past – they've so much presence, live they're great, but they didn't have a song to save their lives. But lately, say 'Pride (In The Name Of Love)' was a good song. The whole thing makes sense. You could sit down at a piano or with a guitar and play it and it'd sound great.'

Paul Cleary, former member of The Blades, U2 contemporaries in the late 1970s, *Hot Press Yearbook* (1986).

'People say we take ourselves too seriously and I might have to plead guilty to that. But really, I don't take myself seriously, we don't take ourselves seriously – but we do take the music seriously.'

Bono, *Hot Press* (18 August 1983).

'A lot of our songs had those strange twists – "turn left at Greenland"! Sometimes they didn't work out, it has to be said.'

Edge, in *U2 By U2* (2006).

'The privilege of walking on that stage knowing you've got twenty-five years of great material, you've got three other people that you've known for thirty years, you've got a crew most of whom you've known for twenty years – all those things add up. And whatever hardships or difficulties you might experience, that's about as good as it gets.'

Adam Clayton, *Mojo* (July 2005).

'We might have the most elastic audience when you think of what we've gone through in the last five years. As long as the songs are good they'll go with us all the way. When we start writing shit songs then we'll know it's over.'

Bono, *Propaganda* (1988).

'What happened to the whole punk thing – just getting up and doing what you feel? I'm into the spirit, not into the musicianship.'

Larry Mullen Jr, *Modern Drummer* (1986).

'[Music] is my escape from work. It's where I have the luxury to dream.'

Bono on Bono (2005).

'You could see that while Bono had his appeal, Edge, in context, was the guy who made the group happen. He was very innovative, creative and had a very different sound from most of the other bands at the time ... Bono would be more inclined to look at things in a different light, probably in more of an aesthetic, ambitious, creative way. Bono had the vision and art, Edge the unique sound and style.'

Joe O'Herlihy, in Diana Scrimgeour, *U2 Show* (2004).

'The indie music scene was a bunch of lies sold to people. It made our life in U2 a lot less interesting and a lot more lonely – even just in terms of who we were sharing hotels with ... We were smart enough to go to America and bypass that. We took a few blows for that and a few connected.'

Bono, *Cara* (June 2005).

'They're very ambitious for the music ... I think they feel a responsibility to the audience not to be crap. That's probably what drives them more than anything else. They're intensely competitive ... not for the sake of competition but because they want to go on being good.'

Paul McGuinness, *Hot Press* (4 October 2006).

'You're not going to complain if Martin Scorsese makes *Raging Bull* and then moves on to *The King of Comedy*. It's just the subject matter of the work that dictates the way you present it. The album cover, the tour, the way the stage is dressed, the way you are dressed – you're following the logic of the music. I am amazed that some groups seem to stay interested, playing the same music for ten or twenty years. But our music has been changing since 1980. The change between the *War* album and *The Unforgettable Fire* is as dramatic as this [*Achtung Baby/Zooropa*]. We follow the subject matter.'

Bono, *Q* (January 1993).

'I work with Edge the most – he has the best ears for hearing detail. What he can hear just amazes me, and he is always right. I've never seen him make a wrong choice about anything to do with engineering ... With him the brain, the heart and the ears are involved and I think that is what makes him so unique.'

Cheryl Engels, recording quality controller, in Diana Scrimgeour, *U2 Show* (2004).

'I just hope that when it's all over for U2 that in some way we made the light a little bit brighter. Maybe just tore off a corner of the darkness.'

Bono, *Propaganda* (1987).

'We work in an unorthodox fashion and regularly drive producers, engineers, assistant engineers, studio managers and anybody else who happens to be around to distraction. Because it's not one person you have to deal with, it's four people and it takes an awful lot of stamina and a lot of understanding to work with us.'

Larry Mullen Jr, in *U2 By U2* (2006).

'They used to say about U2 that we had an anti-dance stance, music to fall over to – which I thought was funny. I remember in an American club on an early tour, Bono, after a few bevvies, was persuaded to go on the floor and the DJ put on 'Out Of Control', and not only did everybody leave the floor, but he couldn't dance to it either.'

Edge, *Hot Press* (March 1987).

'Over the years, many things have been brought in from sound-check recordings. On *All That You Can't Leave*

Behind, there was an amazing warren that I'm not sure even made it to the finish. And Edge is always knocking them out at home. He's the archivist of the band.'

Daniel Lanois, record producer, in Diana Scrimgeour, *U2 Show* (2004).

'The walls needed underpinning, we had to put down new foundations or the house would fall down. In fact, it was falling down all around us. We were running up hotel bills and we had professional people, the U2 crew, staring at our averageness and scratching their heads and wondering if maybe they'd have been better off working for Bruce Springsteen. We came face to face with our limitations as a group on a lot of levels, playing and songwriting ... Larry and Adam were just anxious: "Stop messing around with all this electronica, let's get back to doing what we do. Because all this experimental stuff isn't working very well, is it? And, by the way, *Clockwork Orange* was shite." There was a bit of that going on. "Did somebody say we were a rock band?" As you'd be walking down the corridor, you'd overhear that kind of remark.'

Bono, in *U2 By U2* (2006).

'I've got friends who think that U2 are the roots of all evil. We argue about it, I stick this on, and they lose. 'Bad' is U2 at their best because it's so unselfconscious. Some people think it's too sentimental, but my first feelings when I hear someone say that is a slight tinge of pity.'

Danny McNamara, singer with Embrace, *Q* (August 2006).

'They knew a great deal about what they wanted to do, musically. Before Edge, all guitarists based their riffs around the blues ... but Edge had this jangle thing, and since then that's what his guitar is. In the studio, the line of communication was quite clear. Bono could tell Edge what he wanted to do and Edge knew what he meant. What Bono wants is very important, but Bono couldn't do what he wants without Edge to translate it. Separately they're great. Together they're unbeatable.'

Barry Devlin, director, early producer and member of Horslips, in Diana Scrimgeour, *U2 Show* (2004).

'Maybe 'great' is what happens when 'very good' gets tired. We kind of out-stared the average, it blinked first and 'One' arrived.'

Bono, in *U2 By U2* (2006).

'From very early on, it became clear to us that we had no idea about songwriting technique. Our way into songwriting was to dream it up. We'd try to imagine how others might do the song, The Clash or Lennon or The Jam. Instinct was everything for us, and it really still is.'

Edge, *Los Angeles Times* (August 2004).

'It must have been soul-destroying to work so hard and put so much in and then have these two guys say, "Well, actually it's not ready." It took grace to respond by saying, "Maybe you're right." And that's all it is: maybe you're right. You take your chances. It says a lot about both of them that they were prepared to listen to a bass player and a drummer who have difficulty playing in time.'

Larry Mullen Jr, on Bono and Edge and the writing of songs for *How To Dismantle An Atomic Bomb*, in *U2 By U2* (2006).

'We're like a virus that surrounds you with too many permutations and combinations till you just don't know where to turn.'

Bono, on U2 in the recording studio, in *U2 By U2* (2006).

'My view of their music is a personal view, inasmuch as they're highly likely to have a personal view of my music ... I know they loved 'High On Emotion' ... I don't think that the success of U2 should rely completely on the music. Some of the music is excellent, some of it is pretty indifferent...'

Chris de Burgh, *Chris de Burgh – the Authorised Biography* (1996).

'Songwriting by accident is so important, and the getting to the place where that can happen or, as we say, getting to the place where God can walk through the room ... If you know what great is, you know you're a long way from it.'

Bono on Bono (2005).

'On a musical level, I still don't believe U2 has reached its peak and there are a lot of things for us to do. I look forward to that challenge and without that goal there is no point in continuing ... I'd like to think that whatever happens [next] will be better not bigger.'

Larry Mullen Jr, *Rhythm* magazine (1993).

'[U2] songs now sound like the lowest common denominator of an infinitely more polished unit, whereas twelve or seventeen years ago, their music was the highest common factor of a quadropoly of intensity that seemed to defy gravity. They know better what they're doing now. They know about pop and its history. They know whom they have to beat to stay ahead of the game. But they no longer have the collective sense of recklessness that made them great.'

John Waters, *The Irish Book Review* (Autumn/Winter, 2006).

'Music is a life or death experience, which it sounds mad to say. Honestly, that's how we felt about it. It wasn't entertainment.'

Bono, *From a Whisper to a Scream,* television series (2000).

"'One' was one of those songs where you get a gift. It just arrived, and we had it down within about fifteen minutes. In those situations, you just have to make sure you don't get your hands all over it and fuck it up.'

Edge, in Jim Irvin and Colin McLear (editors), *The Mojo Collection: The Ultimate Music Companion* (2003).

'Our music is too big to have a roof over its head. The worship of the garage comes from people who never started out in one or can't get out of it. We did.'

Bono, *Vanity Fair* (November 2004).

'U2 songs can come together very fast with everyone in the room and it's all very exciting, and you've got something very quickly. And sometimes it's a very frustrating process ... What I do a lot of times is just try to get a song to the point where it will take flight. There's no formality to it. It's very much a trial and error thing.'

Edge, *Irish Independent* (19 June 2005).

'We were tremendously green, but mixed with a kind of self-assuredness. I remember feeling what we were doing wasn't in isolation. It was part of what Echo and the Bunnymen were doing, what The Teardrop Explodes were doing ... It was about a generation getting a voice.'

Adam Clayton, *Mojo* (July 2005).

'The early material was a bit of a challenge. Twenty years ago, I played with little knowledge of what I was doing. And that is the beauty of those early songs, the parts are kind of obscure, simple and naïve. I wanted to play them again with new confidence but without losing their early magic. It was nice to rewrite a little history.'

Larry Mullen Jr, on playing tracks from *Boy* during the Vertigo tour, in *U2 By U2* (2006).

'Writing songs scares the living daylights out of me.'

Bono, in Niall Stokes, *Into the Heart: The Stories behind Every U2 Song* (2001).

'Our music comes from being around real people in the real world.'

Larry Mullen Jr, *Modern Drummer* (1986).

'We didn't go to art school, we went to Brian Eno.'

Bono on Bono (2005).

'We've never had a problem with influences, although we have this very strong rule that if we like a song we've written because it reminds us of someone else, then we'll get rid of it. If we like it anyway and it always happens to remind us of someone, then we'll keep it ... We've never been shy of influences – everybody borrows from everybody else. And I don't mind people borrowing ideas, as long as they're not just re-hashing and creating pastiches. That just reduces and debases the work.'

Edge, *Q* (September 1993).

'We still feel that our records are as good as anything we've ever done, so our determination to make that be true means we're not willing to take second best ever, and that means driving our engineers and producers completely mad.'

Edge, *Irish Independent* (19 June 2005).

'We had a deep-seated belief that the sprit of the band was true enough and strong enough and imperishable enough to not rely on any obvious guitar sounds or signatures to come through. It would come through, anyway. It would come through a thick prison wall.'

Bono, in *U2 By U2* (2006).

'We haven't written it yet.'

Bono, when asked what his favourite U2 song is, in *Bono on Bono* (2005).

'Had I not got Edge close by ... I would be hopeless. Had I not got Larry and Adam, these melodies would not be grounded.'

Bono on Bono (2005).

'U2's music has many different elements. If someone comes along to a concert and is inspired to join Amnesty that's one part of it, but someone else may feel emotionally over-whelmed by the music, and someone else again may just come along to jump up and down and bop. They're all relevant; they're all important. They're intertwined, and to put emphasis on one element is wrong.'

Larry Mullen Jr, *Musician* (1 October, 1987).

'In keeping with the punk ethic of non-musicianship, our early songwriting was characterised by a lack of virtuosity. So we would always try and bolt on an unexpected bit, some sort of change that would in some way get us over the fact that we weren't doing it very skilfully.'

Adam Clayton, in *U2 By U2* (2006).

'Songwriting really is a mysterious process ... because we're asking people to expose themselves. It's like open-heart surgery in some way. You're looking for real, raw emotions, and you don't find that by sticking to the rules.'

Bono, *Los Angeles Times* (August 2004).

'If I'm in the studio I will listen to what the band are doing but I am a very poor judge of material that is only halfway finished. The band all know that, so they don't bother playing it to me because it's a waste of time. It's embarrassing to say that but it's true.'

Paul McGuinness, *Propaganda* (1991).

'If we stay in small clubs we'll develop small minds, and then we'll start making small music.'

Bono, *Trouser Press* (May 1983).

'Whenever rock music strays too far from the single, it gets into heavy water. Deep shit. Sure, we love meandering, but if we're honest, that's what it's all about. This band still has the ambition, the audacity, to take on pop music. We want to make an album where it's as experimental as it is disciplined, where it is one sound and yet we stretch that sound to include pure pop and violence. So it still seems like there's more work for us to do.'

Bono, *Mojo* (July 2005).

'Bono said he loved Joy Division? He loved them too much; loving is one thing, copying is another! Their last one sounded just like 'Isolation', I thought.'

Peter Hook, bass player with New Order, *Hot Press Yearbook* (2007).

'Over the years, we never thought we were that interesting, so we were always trying to find other things to do with our sound or our personality. Put it through the mincer in a way … A new found appreciation for pure melody – that seems to be what we're all interested in at the moment.'

Edge, *Q* (January 2007).

'Being a singer is a terrible responsibility. I sometimes get the odd twinge that I wouldn't mind playing lead guitar, just like a couple of notes, but that's as near as I would want to get to the front. It looks so frightening being the singer, especially from where I am.'

Larry Mullen Jr, *Melody Maker* (14 March 1987).

'There are moments when you hear the voice crack and you think, "This has gone too far. I should be treating my voice with a bit more care." But most of the time I would come back from those marches, rallies, meetings or conference rooms and arrive on the stage two feet taller. I'm floating because of what could come out of all of this ... I feel like I've been carried by people's prayers. And it hasn't hurt me at all. I'm in top shape ... My voice has never been as strong. How could that be? It's crazy.'

Bono, in *U2 By U2* (2006).

'The spirit that we found that was always in our music is stronger now. It's exciting for a rock and roll band to strip itself right down, to take off all recognisable signs and just bash away and say, "This is still us."'

Bono, *Rolling Stone* (9 March 1989).

'Our band has certainly reached the end of where we've been at for the last couple of albums. I want to see what else we can do with it, take it to the next level. I think that's what we've got to do. We're going to continue to be a band, but maybe the rock will have to go; maybe the rock has to get a lot harder. But whatever it is, it's not going to stay where it is. I would like to do a couple of tunes in that direction, with just a lot of space around the voice, I'd like to strip things down; that's something I'd be very interested in at the moment.'

Bono, talking up a new musical direction for U2, *Jo Wylie Show*, BBC Radio 1 (January 2007).

'I still don't think it's as good as 'Stairway to Heaven'.'

Adam Clayton on 'One', *Q* (September 1993).

Lyrics

There's little doubt that through Bono, as the primary lyricist, U2 are hidebound to what he wants to write about, what his concerns are and, er, what he comes up with on the spot. One or two of the band's record producers have expressed bemusement (this is an understatement) of how the lyrics are left until last, with Bono occasionally making them up as he's singing into the microphone. Certainly, in the main there are no obvious singer-songwriter structures to the lyrics. That said, Bono has latterly found the knack to come up with the goods, in particular when he's writing from the basis of his own experience. A personal perspective is where he's at and what he's good at, then, but it's possibly more true to say that he sings words better than writes them.

'I tell Rushdie that, on the plane to Italy last month, I was reading his collection *Imaginary Homelands*. When I came to his essay on Raymond Carver I was struck by a line from Carver's poem 'Suspenders' that Rushdie quoted about the "quiet that comes to a house where nobody can sleep". It

clearly inspired Bono's line in 'Ultraviolet (Light My Way)':
"There is a silence that comes to our house when no one can
sleep." When I mentioned the reference to Bono he said, "*Ah,
shit*! I didn't realise that! I must have read it and forgotten it.
I thought that was my line." He grumbled for a minute and
then said with mock sadness, "I thought I was the genius."
"Subconscious plagiarism," Rushdie smiles. "Happens to all
of us all the time."'

Bill Flanagan, *U2 at the End of the World* (1995).

'It amazes me when people tell me they played it at their
wedding or for comfort at a funeral. I go to myself, "Are you
crazy? It's about breaking up."'

Bono, on 'One', *Los Angeles Times* (August 2004).

'Bono does have difficulty in sitting down and actually
writing words out – he sings whatever comes out. It's a very
painful process for him – I'm sure he'd admit this – he puts
himself through a lot of hardship to come out with what he
feels are his best lyrics.'

Steve Lillywhite, U2 record producer, *Propaganda* (1985).

'I found Niall Stokes' article on U2 very amusing. Describing
the song 'Elevation', Mr Stokes said it "captures well the
murky terrain inhabited by a writer struggling with the
attempt to make art of his or her experience, and the natural
proclivity of creativity, spirituality and sex". Mr Stokes is so
right, of course, the song does capture the murky terrain of a
writer struggling. Bono was struggling so much with this
song that he came up with lyrics such as "mole/digging in a
hole/digging up my soul now/going down, excavation". Now,
I'm no expert, but these lyrics seem a little, oh I don't know,

uninspiring to say the least, although they seem to have been quite inspirational to Mr Stokes ... Maybe a simpler description would have sufficed, like, say, "Shit song."'

Letter to *Hot Press* (24 January 2007).

'This song was written literally on the day the Omagh bomb went off, right then. Nobody could actually believe it ... It would be hard to describe to people who are not Irish what that felt like that day. It was certainly the lowest day of my life, outside personal losses.'

Bono, on 'Peace on Earth', in Niall Stokes, *Into the Heart: The Stories behind Every U2 Song* (2001).

'Probably the most bitter U2 song ever. Somebody told me they thought it was the exact opposite of 'Imagine'.'

Edge, on 'Elevation', *Mojo* (December 2000).

'It's lovely to have a song ['The Fly'] with such undertones of evil coming out.'

Brian Eno, *Propaganda* (1991).

'It was as if my whole life was in that song. Electronic blues death rattle. It takes the cliché insult 'motherfucker' and turns it into something raw and confessional. It went through some bizarre titles – Mothership, Oedipussy...'

Bono, on the song 'Mofo', from *Pop*, in *U2 By U2* (2006).

'There were a lot of unfinished lyrics that were written in five minutes instead of five hours ... The first two lines of 'Where The Streets Have No Name' were just written on the mic – "I want to run I want to hide, I want to tear down the walls that hold me inside." It's like teenage poetry! The idea behind the song ... that you can transcend where you are, the idea of music as a sacrament is so powerful, but it's this fucking inane couplet.'

Bono, *Q* (July 2001).

'If people imagined that all our songs were autobiographical, they would have a very strange impression of what we were like.'

Edge, *Q* (September 1993).

'That was Edge's phrase. Edge said it and I wrote a song around it. One thing I know and I must say this to you – Coca Cola it is not.'

Bono, on 'I Still Haven't Found What I'm Looking For', *Hot Press* (December 1988).

'They have not yet matched The Beatles. Bono is so bright, so full of ideas that he certainly has the potential to do so, but lyrically he has not written an 'Eleanor Rigby' or 'I Am The Walrus'.'

Salman Rushdie, in Bill Flanagan, *U2 at the End of the World* (1995).

'It's a little odd for me, when people walk up and say, "We played 'One' at our wedding – thank you so much." Did you ever hear the lyrics?! The spleen and the bile, and you walked down the aisle to that one, did you?! ... It's proof of what Larry, Edge and Adam have always believed – no one listens to the lyrics.'

Bono, *Mojo* (July 2005).

Concerts

Say what you want about their records, say what you want about their music, say what you want about their personalities, say what you want about what they say, but when U2 take to the stage, there is rarely a major debate: the title of Best Rock Band In The World is but a heartbeat away from the truth. Early U2 gigs (and we mean early – as far back as when they were a support band) were a mixture of hot and cold, hit and miss, mime and misfortune, but from the time they started headlining, they were able to translate what was in their heads into what they were able to do on stage (budgets permitting). For a while, it seemed as if they were falling over themselves in trying to best their previous tours, a matter that came very much unstuck during the PopMart shows. But they stripped things back for subsequent outings, developed a leaner approach stylistically as well as musically, and came out of the traps like greyhounds after a hare. And say what you want in particular about Bono (and, yes, we know you will) but only a bigot will deny that he makes for a bona-fide great rock-star front man.

'U2's longevity in the transitory world of rock music is unique. They are the only band of their generation to have retained their original line-up, to be still composing and releasing their own music and still be among the handful of performers able to sell out a world stadium tour. They are a band with a conscience and a message. Their particular combination of heart, mind, intellect and spirit makes for a thrilling and challenging live performance.'

Diana Scrimgeour, in the foreword to her book, *U2 Show* (2004).

'I don't want to see all that ZooTV crap. I like U2 ... they've written some really good songs, but Bono in those Fly shades – fuckin' spare me!'

Bob Geldof, in B.P. Fallon, *U2 Faraway So Close* (1994). Geldof later went to see a ZooTV show in London. His verdict. 'It was expensive bollox, signifying fuck all...'

'During 'Walk On', we rolled the names of all the people who were missing after the 9/11 attacks and that was a powerful cathartic moment and an amazing thing to be part of. The wounds were still raw and an audience has to really trust you to let you push certain buttons. And those audiences did, they trusted us and they went there with us.'

Adam Clayton on U2 playing New York's Madison Square Garden following 9/11, in *U2 By U2* (2006).

'The lights came on during 'Where the Streets Have No Name' and there must have been ten thousand people with tears running down their faces. And I told them they looked beautiful, which became the line in 'City Of Blinding Lights'.'

Bono, on U2 playing New York's Madison Square Garden following 9/11, in *U2 By U2* (2006).

'We've always had intensity and a sense of being servants of the moment. But I don't remember us being this loose and this tight. It takes both to be really great. This might sound odd, but I've never looked forward to a U2 show before. I remember sometimes not being able to speak before a show, and going to quiet places trying to reserve energy. Now, mostly I wake up in the morning, going, "There's some people I wanna meet tonight and one of them's myself."'

Bono, on Vertigo shows, *Mojo* (July 2005).

'Thank you, Sydney.'

Edge, at U2's sell-out concert in Telstra Dome – in Melbourne, *Irish Mail on Sunday* (26 November 2006).

'A lot of humour, a lot of theft, a lot of scamming – all the things that rock 'n' roll was always good at.'

Paul McGuinness, on ZooTV, in B.P. Fallon, *U2 Faraway So Close* (1994).

'If you thought we were over the top in the past, check this out.'

Bono, on ZooTV, *NME* (13 June 1992).

'People can see through pretend – if a band can't do it for real, then people shouldn't go to see them. Emotion is everything.'

Bono, *Boston Rock* magazine (December 1980).

'If Bono had wanted to cancel the show, of course, we would have. But knowing Bono's character, I assumed he would want to play. He believes in including people in whatever's going on. I think he believed the right place for him to be was on the stage, revealing his grief in the music and having it witnessed by an audience. I don't think he knows any other way. I don't think having a quiet night, keeping vigil, would have been Bono's way.'

Edge, on Bono's way of coping with the death of his father on 21 August 2001, the day of U2's third show at London's Earl's Court, in *U2 By U2* (2006).

'In a place like Slane, where you have a crucible of people, a gig can be a sacramental event.'

Bono, on U2 playing at Slane Castle a few days after his father died, in *U2 By U2* (2006).

'Their live shows have always been honest. We took a lot of criticism about that on ZooTV and PopMart, about whether it was honest, or whether it was cynical ... But I think there's always been an honesty there that the fans have latched on to. U2 have always been consistent in a number of things: the quality of the music, the quality of the live show and their commitment to human rights. I think that as long as the message is consistent, people will listen. And the honesty with which it's delivered is important.'

Jake Kennedy, U2 director of PopMart, in Diana Scrimgeour, *U2 Show* (2004).

'We pissed ourselves.'

Edge, on the night in Scandinavia when Zooropa's motorised Lemon pod malfunctioned, leaving the band stuck inside, *Q* (November 2002).

'Bono is adored. He dangerously treads the fine line between being an adulated rock star and parodying that role. He controls fights and calms down a stage invasion. He's never sure whether to patronise the audience for their stupidity, understand and gee them on, cool them down or join in. In the end, he does it all and more. Acting, hurting, fighting. His performance is unruly but riveting.'

Review of a U2 gig in Cork, *NME* (February 1980).

'To me a rock 'n' roll concert is 3-D. It's a physical thing – it's rhythm for the body. It's a mental thing in that it should be intellectually challenging. But it's also a spiritual thing, because it's a community, it's people agreeing on something even if it's only for an hour and a half.'

Bono, *Wall Street Journal* (2 April 1985).

'Those early Dandelion Market concerts, those McGonagle's concerts were actually quite similar to where we are now ... Surrealism – Irish surrealism, those ideas that ZooTV plays with, we were playing them back then, but we never knew what we were doing.'

Bono, in John Waters, *Race of Angels – the Genesis of U2* (1994).

'A concert is the most authentic form of music. Records were invented a long time after music. Ask Beethoven.'

Adam Clayton, *Best* (October 1984).

'The weather conditions were horrible and the gig, complete with filming and recording, should have been called off. It was scary, it was very tense. Financially, everything they had was riding on the filming and recording of the gig. To have pulled the plug on it would have been a disaster for them. Instead, they managed to make magic from all the adversity. It really was magic. The tougher the going got, the better they got. Always.'

Ellen Darst, Principle Management employee from 1983–93, on the Red Rocks concert, in Diana Scrimgeour, *U2 Show* (2004).

'Things get out of hand up there. I experience everything in slow motion. The crowd, the group, everything seems slowed down. Like a dream. It's only when I come off I realise it was me that was fired up, speeding on it all. Takes me hours to come back down.'

Bono, *NME* (6 June 1987).

'The record was hailed as being back to basics, which it wasn't. And the tour was described as a minimalist production, which, of course, it really wasn't. It is all relative, and compared to *Pop* anything would seem back to basics.'

Edge, on *All That You Can't Leave Behind* album/Elevation tour, in *U2 By U2* (2006).

'People are screaming their souls out, they're screaming for themselves, because their lives are wrapped up in those songs. So one starts, and then they go off. You see, it's not about us, it's about them. If we weren't great, they wouldn't be there the next time. That's just the way it is. People are discerning and tickets cost money ... The U2 audience does tend to be smarter than your average bear. They're not like a bunch of arty-farty types, they're not intellectuals, but they're thinking people.'

Bono on Bono (2005).

'There was this notion that the irony, with which the project was supposedly imbued, would translate. But it didn't. No matter how many times we tried to explain, there were still plenty of people who thought the tour was sponsored by Kmart and McDonald's. I don't think people were stupid, they just didn't want irony in rock 'n' roll and they certainly didn't want it from U2. As a campaign that took a lot out of everyone and doesn't have a lot of happy memories.'

Paul McGuinness, on PopMart, *Mojo* (July 2005).

'Gee, those guys have so much integrity, I just can't believe that they have Kmart sponsoring their tour.'

Sheryl Crow, on PopMart, in Bill Flanagan, *U2 at the End of the World* (1995).

'I don't like music unless it has a healing effect. I don't like it when people leave concerts still feeling edgy. I want people to leave our concerts feeling positive, a bit more free.'

Bono, *NME* (26 February 1983).

'This tour feels like the completion of what we are as a group. The band has a mannish quality that you wouldn't fuck with, you know.'

Bono, on the Elevation tour, *Q* (March 2002).

'I have moments of rage when I think about how stupid we were to allow ourselves to be talked into booking a tour before *Pop* was finished. Sometimes, you can get caught up in a certain madness, where you believe you can do anything. We were wrong. There may well have been a certain amount of arrogance. There was certainly arrogance around us ... Had we been great, people would have got it. I really believe that. Because we would have overshadowed the production. But because we didn't have our act together, the production swallowed us up, for the first three or four months. By the middle of that tour, it was a different thing, because we'd learned the songs, were playing them better than we'd played them on record. But no one remembers that. They just remember the first night and the lemon. Which is okay. We live to tell the tale.'

Larry Mullen Jr, on PopMart, *Mojo* (July 2005).

'People say that playing live is stunting – you get bored, you get bogged down. But for us, every time we go on stage there is a real atmosphere of anticipation within the band. There are no two nights which could be said to be the same – the set may be the same, but the audience is different and our approach to each audience varies.'

Edge, radio interview on Boston's WBCN (April 1983).

'One guy popped his glass eye out, then there was a guy who'd killed his best friend in a car wreck who gave this heart-rending confession which instantly cut to a woman taking her top off. It was a brilliant mind-fuck.'

Willie Williams, U2 set designer, on the Video Confessional Booth during the 1992 ZooTV tour, *Q* (November 2002).

'Bono phoning the White House was a nice touch but he would only ever get through to the operator. In the course of the whole [ZooTV] tour, I don't think he managed to strike up a relationship with the operator. If you know Bono, that's got to be some tough cookie.'

Adam Clayton, in *U2 By U2* (October 2006).

'U2 are involved in Live Aid because it's more than money, it's music ... but it's also a demonstration to the politicians and policy makers that men, women and children will not walk by other men, women and children as they lie, bellies swollen, starving to death for the sake of a cup of grain and water. For the price of Star Wars, the Mx missile offensive-defence budgets, the deserts of Africa could be turned into fertile lands. The technology is with us. The technocrats are not. Are we part of a civilisation that protects itself by investing in life ... or investing in death?'

Official U2 statement to the British media on the band's involvement in Live Aid (1985).

'U2 seized the moment. They were just brilliant in that big stadium environment ... Not many people make the transition into being the big stadium band. And U2 went for it and won.'

Midge Ure, on U2's performance at Live Aid, 10th Anniversary BBC special (1995).

'One of the great ironies of [our] concerts is that our songs are very intimate: incredible intimacies shared with people you've never met. And I wouldn't trust that. Who would trust that? That's a very bizarre way to live your life.'

Bono on Bono (2005).

'We came off stage after Live Aid and we thought we had really blown it. We thought that the idea of doing 'Bad' really hadn't worked, because Bono went into the audience. That was fine, but as everyone saw who was watching the TV coverage, it was like nothing he wanted to do seemed to happen for him: he couldn't get into the audience, he couldn't get the person he wanted out of the audience onto the stage, it was turning into a real embarrassment – a real disaster.'

Edge, promotional interview for Island Records (1987).

'Bono's journey really meant something, it carried the emotion of the day to people. So his performer's instinct was right. Again.'

Adam Clayton, on Live Aid, in *U2 By U2* (2006).

'I really thought we were crap. But looking back, as I did a week later, I started to see what it was. It was the sense of real, total jeopardy, which is always very exciting for a live event, and Bono's complete determination to make physical contact with the crowd.'

Edge, on Live Aid, in *U2 By U2* (2006).

'The broad strokes, the high points are the things that people remember ... it has been Bono's persona on stage that people have carried away with them. The unfortunate side of that is not that he has the ability to lose control, but that it is all the fans remember. That's a very one-dimensional view of the band ...'

Edge, promotional interview for Island Records (December 1984).

'Not bad for a bunch of Paddies.'

Larry Mullen Jr, on the news that U2's Italian concert in Reggio Emelia attracted in excess of 170,000 people, making it the highest ever attendance for a paying audience at a one-act concert (i.e. other than festivals and free shows), *Propaganda* (1997).

'We can be in the middle of the worst gig of our lives, but when we go into that song, everything changes. The audience is on its feet, singing along with every word. It's like God suddenly walks through the room. It's the point where craft ends and spirit begins. How else can you explain it?'

Bono, on 'Where The Streets Have No Name', *Los Angeles Times* (August 2004).

'I can't remember anything more excruciating than those Sarajevo link-ups. It was like throwing a bucket of cold water over everybody. You could see your audience going, what the fuck are these guys doing?'

Larry Mullen Jr, on the ZooTV tour's incorporation of satellite link-ups to a television studio in Sarajevo, *Q* (November 2002).

'There were some great nights on PopMart. But there were some I would like to wipe from my memory. It's a bit of a sobering experience to play to a half-full stadium ... or less! The worst of all was Tampa Florida, 20,000 people in a stadium built for 75,000 ... And then we got to Cologne and there's 29,000 people in a 60,000-capacity stadium.'

Edge, in *U2 By U2* (2006).

'Loosely, ZooTV and PopMart could be said to articulate statements about the post-modern world – describing that world back to itself as a perilous pleasure dome of seemingly infinite images and information, the accelerated accumulation of which might seem to threaten our perceptions, free will and fundamental human feelings. In this much, the U2 show is about acting out a passion play of good versus evil in a very blatant way. Why else might Bono, during ZooTV, achieve such a bravura performance as the Devil – played, incidentally, not as a swaggering satanic Mick Jagger, sinewy in black, but rather as a sentimental old impresario, virtually exhausted by the suffering he has given to the world. Occurring towards the end of the concert, Bono's extraordinary performance as the satanic creator of mass media comprises one of the most sophisticated theatrical statements to be made by a rock show ... The scale and complexity of ZooTV – its astonishing use of technology and the ergonomics of a concert stage – is literally breathtaking.'

Michael Bracewell, in Diana Scrimgeour, *U2 Show* (2004).

'There were the inevitable post mortems and we came to some conclusions. Mine would have been: don't bite off more than you can chew.'

Paul McGuinness, giving his final comment on the PopMart tour, in *U2 By U2* (2006).

'We are just not worth it. Save your money and see lots of other bands instead.'

Paul McGuinness, advising fans on hearing that ticket touts and some ticket agencies were reselling tickets for U2's sold-out show at London's Earl's Court, *Q* (July 1992).

'A great rock show can be a transcendent event. A crap one on the other hand can feel like a funeral – your own! But it's an extraordinary thing to get seventy thousand people or seven thousand people to agree on anything. I mean, we've all been to really doglike events ... In a club you can feel as far from the singer as in a stadium, depending on the mentality of the singer. It's not about physical proximity.'

Bono on Bono (2005).

'Thanks for giving us a great life. I mean that, actually. Thank you very much.'

Bono, on stage at Manchester's MEN venue (12 August 2001).

'Taste is the enemy of art.'

'Watch more TV.'

'Believe everything.'

'A liar won't believe anyone else.'

'Celebrity is a job.'

'Remember what you dream.'

'Enjoy the surface.'

'Ambition bites the nails of success.'

'It's your world, you can change it.'

'Contradiction is balance.'

'I'd like to teach the world to sing.'

'Call your mother.'

'Ask the right questions.'

'Everything not forbidden is compulsory.'

'Cry more often.'

'React or die.'

'Everything you know is wrong.'

'The future is a fantasy.'

'Death is a career move.'

'A friend is someone who lets you help.'

'Celery is rhubarb's ugly sister.'

'Guilt is not of God.'

'Nobody is promised a tomorrow.'

'Pig wife Japan sucker bomb now pussy.'

'Nobody move and nobody get hurt.'

'Everyone's a racist except you.'

'Work is the blackmail of survival.'

'Be gentle with me.'

'Talk to strangers.'

'It could never happen here.'

'Silence=Death.'

'Service not included.'

Some of the soundbites communicated via video walls to fans during the ZooTV tour.

'In the most glorious way, ZooTV spiralled beyond the control of any of the individuals involved. Expecting anything and surprised by nothing, all we could do was keep running until the tour finally came to an end in Tokyo almost two full years later ... I can say with absolute confidence that there will never be another rock tour like it.'

Willie Williams, U2 show designer, on the ZooTV tour, in Diana Scrimgeour, *U2 Show* (2004).

'When you watch U2 [in an arena-sized venue] they build something much bigger than themselves. All U2's songs are about love in one way or another. That's a very courageous thing to do. They let go of themselves and when they do a song like 'One' the feeling is unbelievable. I saw seven U2 shows last year and I could not see them enough. Their shows are the only shows I've ever seen that work in an arena. Everything else is bullshit or a trip to the circus.'

Elvis Costello, *Word* (April 2003).

'After each show, the group usually has a review of the show ... Sometimes we listen to the tapes from Joe's [O'Herlihy] sound desk, or view the videotapes of the show. This way, if there are small problems they are dealt with and the show remains at 100 per cent. Every night they play, U2 always give more than seems possible, and it will always be like that. Their perception is that you should come away from a U2 show remembering everything you've seen and heard.'

Dennis Sheehan, U2 tour manager 1983–present, in Diana Scrimgeour, *U2 Show* (2004).

'It was a difficult decision for us, because we've always tried to create a feeling of intimacy in any show. People said we couldn't do it in arenas, and I really believe we did. When it came to stadiums, we really had to make the move, because if we didn't it meant playing to twenty nights in an arena, which we just couldn't face. Bruce Springsteen seems able to do that and retain his sanity, but any more than about six shows in one town and we start going totally wacky. It becomes like a job.'

Edge, on the reasons behind moving from theatre shows to stadia concerts, *Rolling Stone* (10 March 1988).

'Bono was wearing boots and he climbed on to the roof of the stage, a stunt he pulled a few times, a very dangerous thing to do. Nevertheless, it grabbed the attention of the fans. They

[U2] were very determined, and you could tell they were going to the top one way or the other. I don't think they particularly enjoyed being one of the support acts, but they also had the humility to realise the fact that everyone has to start somewhere ... One thing that did strike myself and my band was that, at the end of U2's show, the crowd were left in a fairly aggressive mood. We looked out at the audience and we saw a weirdness that we had never seen before in one of my potential audiences. It really disturbed me, so I had to rethink the beginning of my show.'

Chris de Burgh, on an open-air concert in Germany in May 1985, in *Chris de Burgh – the Authorised Biography* (1996).

'I really believe it is my job to attack the distance between performer and audience. From climbing speaker stacks to stage diving, it is all the same thought. And, if I may be immodest, U2 have reinvented the rock show with that in mind several times, from the B-stage for ZooTV to the heart on Elevation. Now the B-stage is ubiquitous, but I had been trying to do that since the mid-eighties.'

Bono, in *U2 By U2* (2006).

'When people bought the tickets.'

Bono, on the most unexpected moment of the ZooTV tour, *Q* (January 1993).

'I lost my senses completely. Somebody could have died at that concert, it was a real sickener for me. It's meant a total re-evaluation of what we are about live. We don't need to use a battering ram. It has to be down to the music.'

Bono, on his misplaced antics at the Los Angeles' Sports Arena concert on 17 June 1983, *Rolling Stone* (July 1983).

'Part political rally, part gospel tent, part Las Vegas.'

Bono, describing the Vertigo tour, *Cara* (June 2005).

'Larry was pretty much against it. He thought we were exploiting other people's misery for entertainment. Bono definitely felt we were shining a light on something important.'

Paul McGuinness, on the Zooropa link up with Sarajevo, in *U2 By U2* (2006).

'We were playing a rock 'n' roll show and it was lots of fun, and although the political stuff was serious it was done with a smile. Then suddenly seeing video footage of people being bombarded and a satellite link-up with people in Sarajevo saying, "We're being killed, please come and help us." That was really hard to watch and listen to ... I remember saying to Bono, "I don't know if I can handle this any more..." He just pushed through. He said, "I want to do this and I'm going to do it."'

Larry Mullen Jr, on the Zooropa link up with Sarajevo, in *U2 By U2* (2006).

'Live by satellite every night you had the extraordinary spectacle at a rock gig of reality trampling all over art. And then the band would try to recover.'

Bono, on the Zooropa link up with Sarajevo, in *U2 By U2* (2006).

'There is an argument that says we now live in a world of too much culture – of too much of everything, in fact, moving from one form of excess to another. Under such conditions, the awkwardness and jagged edges so necessary to genuine cultural progress become blunted and dull. And the confrontation of such excess, perhaps, is the ultimate message from the visual spectacle of U2's live performances: that in a world where rebellion itself is so often commodified by multinational corporations and communications networks, then the organic power of popular culture must derive from a conversation to which anybody can contribute, as a democracy without frontiers and an art form free of the gallery.'

Michael Bracewell, in Diana Scrimgeour, *U2 Show* (2004).

Stage Sets and Shows

We remember a time when all U2 had on stage as part of the set-up was a hideous makeshift logo. Gradually, the stage sets developed, sometimes into streamlined artefacts – as much a part of the concert as the music – and sometimes into over-designed behemoths that often threatened to cut the stage from underneath them. Ambition, as Bono once wrote, bites the nails of success, and there were also times when U2 stage shows proved just how clever they were. Of course, they employed all the right people, to whom they delegated/traded ideas, but experience tells you that without a sense of ambition nothing gets achieved.

'At that time, it was world beating – and spectacular. And I remember the effect it had on audiences who just stood there and gaped. I remember one of the things I liked hearing most at the time – and I heard it over and over again – would be people saying to me, "It's too much to take in – there's far too much going on to absorb!" and that kind of overload was absolutely the intention behind the show.'

Paul McGuinness, on the ZooTV tour, *Hot Press* (4 October 2006).

'Taking a television station on the road, and spending a quarter of a million dollars a day wasn't just a thrill – it was a bit of a worry! I mean, we were burning money, a bonfire of our vanities. But we were at least spending it on our fans. We were risking bankruptcy for an art project.'

Bono, on ZooTV, in *Bono on Bono* (2005).

'ZooTV is the yardstick by which all other stadium shows will be measured.'

Robert Hilburn, *Los Angeles Times* (15 November 1992).

'We've never really thought of ourselves as a rock group but one feels that there are so many uncertainties that in fact anything is possible. One of the main interests in music is combining everything which has become part of the everyday background like TV programmes or cinema. Anything could happen in a kind of transformation where video games sell more than records, and where audio-visual formats are taking precedence over music. Most showbiz people are shit-scared. We find it stimulating.'

Bono, *Propaganda* (1992).

'I like going to the shows. At this stage, I'm a connoisseur.'

Paul McGuinness, *Hot Press* (4 October 2006).

'There will be a good deal of experimentation when the excitement of accidental discoveries is balanced with the death of promising ideas that don't quite work in reality. A year after the initial conversations, having leapt countless hurdles, held the budget together and (just) managed not to kill each other in the process, we finally make it to the delivery table and give birth to the show. Then, after all of this, when everyone has given absolutely everything they have, the tour begins.'

Willie Williams, U2 show designer, on the process involved in piecing together a stage show, in Diana Scrimgeour, *U2 Show* (2004).

'I don't trust a performer who's content on the stage, content with the distance between him or her and the audience ... I want to feel like the person on stage can stop playing a role, jump down, sit on my knee, follow me home, hug me, mug me, borrow money from me, make me breakfast in the morning ... I don't want people to feel comfortable in the relationship. I want to feel like it could snap.'

Bono on Bono (2005).

'Reviews have been generally ecstatic, with the exception of one reviewer whose vibe was: "How could U2 do this to themselves?" Edge was saying today that he's surprised there hasn't been more of that, but generally people seem to be coping with U2's self-destruction very well.'

Willie Williams, U2 show designer, on ZooTV, *Propaganda* (1992).

'I'm not content with the distance between the crowd and the performer. I'm always trying to cross that distance. I'm trying to do it emotionally, mentally, and, where I can, physically. [Live Aid] was an overpowering day ... I was not happy with just playing our songs and getting out of there ... Of course, afterwards, I got a terrible time from the band, I was almost fired ... This was the worst one for them, to leave them for what felt like hours, apparently. Larry told me he was going to stop playing ... Everyone was very annoyed with me, I mean, very annoyed.'

Bono on Bono (2005).

'Initial ideas included a stage resembling a massive record player, a giant clock and, inexplicably, the sound system being suspended inside a giant paper bag. Evidently, it was time to loosen the leash on our collective imagination ... It was Bono who came back with the final piece of the puzzle. He said we should issue a press release saying that U2 were taking a TV station on tour ... This immediately became the only idea that anyone was taking seriously and there was no further mention of giant paper bags from that point onwards.'

Willie Williams, U2 show designer, on the process involved in piecing together the ZooTV stage show, in Diana Scrimgeour, *U2 Show* (2004).

'The last time we took a TV station on the road; this time we are taking a supermarket.'

Bono, on the PopMart tour, *Mojo* (March 1997).

'On a particularly whacked afternoon in the studio, Bono proposed that at some point in this new show the whole band should travel into the crowd inside some kind of vehicle ... He suggested that an oversized mirrorball should descend from the roof of the stage, move out over the audience and spew them onto the B-stage. It is extraordinary to imagine that this was taken seriously, but indeed it was ... Mark Fisher set about turning this deranged fantasy into engineering reality: the world's first (and last) 40-foot-tall self-propelled mirrorball. After this, the addition of a giant cocktail stick and stuffed olive barely raised an eyebrow.'

Willie Williams, U2 show designer, on the PopMart tour, in Diana Scrimgeour, *U2 Show* (2004).

'Audiences are becoming less used to the dynamics of live performance, an observation that drove my proposal to begin U2's Elevation show with the house lights on. The individuals in the audience could see not only the band arrive but themselves, the friends they came with, the rest of the audience and tangibly understand that they were all physically in the same room. They could be fully aware that they were in the same airspace as these people whose photograph they might have seen a million times. It's not a recording, I am really here; this is happening now and it's happening only now. U2's shows remains unpredictable, yet the relationship between the band and the audience is real. On any given night, personal events, local events and global events can steer the emotional direction of a show. If Bono is struggling, it becomes everybody's struggle. If the 'spirit is in the house', a U2 show can amaze, even if you've seen them play a hundred times before.'

Willie Williams, U2 show designer, in Diana Scrimgeour, *U2 Show* (2004).

Awards

Awards? They've nabbed a few in their time. Their road to success started off with winning an award in Limerick, and they haven't really stopped since (although the geographical spread has widened). There was probably a time in the 1990s when they became blasé about yet another Best Band gong (who wouldn't?), but it seems after the genuine scare of *Pop* and the forward thrust of subsequent albums they were only too glad to be on the receiving end of a *Q* Award here and a Grammy there. Where they put them is anyone's guess – perhaps a locked room somewhere in deepest, darkest Dublin? Or a garden shed in one of their homes?

'All I could think of at the time was being impressed enough to feel that they could make some kind of impact on the international music scene. I also wanted to see them going further than they actually were at that time – they were just a baby band.'

Jackie Hayden, *Hot Press* general manager (then marketing manager of major record label CBS), on U2 winning the co-sponsored 1978 Harp Lager/CBS Talent Contest in Limerick, for which he was one of the judges on St Patrick's Day, *Irish Times Magazine* (25 August 2001).

'I remember the significance of us becoming U2 that night, of it just being the four of us. It was a feeling of OK, now we're where we should be, playing our own material and everything is in place. Next week: *Top of the Pops*.'

Adam Clayton, on winning the 1978 Harp Lager/CBS Talent Contest, in *U2 By U2* (2006).

'I don't have a problem with awards of merit going to whomever they are, deeming whatever it is worthy of recognition. But there is so much puffing up of the chest that the Grammys are in some way a significant artistic achievement, which I find offensive. It's stupid to deny the effect of a good performance at the Grammys, but you're not really going along as an artist – you're going along as a performer, as a press item, as a piece of television. And that's really the worst way in which to receive something that is about the merit of your work. For us the balance is the wrong way.'

Adam Clayton, in Bill Flanagan, *U2 at the End of the World* (1995).

'If you think this is going to our heads, it's too late.'

Bono, informing music industry grandees at a star-studded Grammy Awards ceremony at which U2 won all five of the categories in which they had been nominated, *The Independent* (March 2006).

'I'll leave it to others far more knowledgeable than me to talk about U2's music. All I'll say is that, along with millions of others right across the world, I am a huge fan. But I feel a little more qualified to talk about your personal commitment to tackling global poverty and, in particular, to Africa. I know from talking to you how much these causes matter to you. I know as well how knowledgeable you are about the problems we face and how determined you are to do all you can to help overcome them.'

Tony Blair, British Prime Minister, in an open letter to Bono, apropos to Bono being awarded an honorary British knighthood for his services to the music industry and for his humanitarian work (2006).

'It may have escaped Bono's notice in his redoubt in Dalkey or tax bolt-hole in Amsterdam, but there is currently an enquiry going on in Britain into 'cash for honours'. Not for one minute would I suggest that Bono could be implicated in any such alleged scheme, but it is particularly disappointing for many of us who admire his long campaign to help the Third World that he should feel it necessary to accept the discredited currency of the British honours system.'

Letter to *The Irish Times* (30 December 2006).

'The acceptance of an accolade from the British Empire, which is built upon and continues to sustain Third World poverty, excludes Bono from speaking for the poor. Bono provides a smokescreen for the continued rape of Africa ... Bono may feel genuine empathy for the poor of Africa. But if he wishes to improve their lot in life, he should address the issues which have sustained their systemic impoverishment, and not cloud them by talking about easing an illegitimate debt imposed by the World Bank, created specifically to maintain this poverty, and then accepting a knighthood from Queen Elizabeth.'

Letter to *The Irish Times* (30 December 2006).

'Has this man [Bono] not gained enough self-esteem, to say nothing of wealth, in his chosen fields of entertainment and

Third World activism not to need this meaningless bauble? ... God be with the days when being a rock star meant scoffing at the Establishment, not embracing it pathetically.'

Letter in the *Irish Mail on Sunday* (31 December 2006).

'He rubs shoulders with the great and the good wherever he goes. The Pope, Bill Gates, Nelson Mandela, Bill Clinton and George Bush are all delighted to have their pictures taken with Bono for their family albums. So another honour from another state could be expected to pass almost unnoticed. But this isn't just another gong for the mantelpiece. This one is different...

'There is something about the words 'great', 'British' and 'empire' in the same sentence that still raises hackles on this side of the Irish Sea. They're three words that most Irish folk find difficult to string together without a snarl ... Bono should, one strand of the argument runs, tell the Great British Empire to stick the KBE where the sun doesn't shine ... The more moderate view is that Bono should have expressed his gratitude for the thought but turned down the honorary knighthood all the same...

'The vehemence of the reaction is extraordinary. A few years ago, the Vatican bestowed an honour on Bono and there was scarcely a peep of protest from anyone. But at the time he was collecting his award, this country was awash with tales of clerical scandals and cover-ups ... As an eloquent spokesman for the world's most vulnerable people, Bono could have taken a stand and turned down that summons from the Vatican in protest at the rape, torture and incarceration of the poorest and weakest children of his own country. But I can't recall anyone making that suggestion...

'Scandals or no scandals, I bet there would have been uproar if Bono had pleaded a previous engagement on the day of the Vatican ceremony ... An honour for an individual, of course, is just that – recognition of an individual's achievements ... a tribute to endeavours above and beyond the call of duty. Instead of carping and sniping, shouldn't we celebrate the honoured individual rather than obsessing about the origin of the tribute? ... This is the highest honour the British have to bestow. Yes, it's a bit naff and dated, but the only ones who will look small if we make a fuss will be ourselves. So we should accept it with the jaded grace of seasoned recipients, admire the silverware, then stow it on the cistern top of history and forget about it.'

Brenda Power, *The Sunday Times* (31 December 2006).

'You have my permission to call me pretty much anything, Lord of Lords, your demi-Godness, but not Sir ... How much do you think I'd get for this thing in Weirs [Dublin jewellery shop]?'

Bono, on receiving his Honorary Knight Commander of the Most Excellent Order of the British Empire, *Irish Independent* (30 March 2007).

'One of the ancient privileges of being a freeman of the city is the right to graze sheep on open ground. So the next day, Bono and I borrowed a couple of sheep and took them out to eat the grass on St Stephen's Green. It seemed like a good idea at the time.'

Edge, on U2 being given the Freedom of Dublin City, 18 March 2000, in *U2 By U2* (2006).

'I'd trade my right to graze sheep on Stephen's Green for parking my car on a double yellow line any day.'

Bono, in *U2 By U2* (2006).

Weird or What?

Spinal Tap has spoiled it for all of us, but there remains at the heart of every rock band — successful or not — certain items of interest and embarrassment that it might have been wiser not to admit to, or to have done. Of course, certain incidents will never be admitted to outside the inner circle (or the 'Garden of Eden', as writer Bill Flanagan described U2's core of intimates and associates) and that is only right and proper. But the world and lifestyle of a major rock band is by rights a series of weird scenes inside a goldmine, and we can only guess at the amount of money thrown at nominally idiotic pursuits that would usually be beyond the remit of 'normal' folk. And let's be honest — if you had the money and the wherewithal, wouldn't you order a curry from your favourite Delhi restaurant and have it flown over to your mansion by the sea? You would, wouldn't you?

'Over 150 Episcopal churches in the US have begun using U2 music at communion; it's the U2Charist.'

Observer Music Monthly (12 November 2006).

'The Bank of America have irked U2 after film of an employee singing 'One' at a corporate bash appeared on YouTube. Banker Ethan Chandler changed the lyrics to celebrate a recent merger ("It's one bank/One card..."). Cue a legal letter from Bono's lawyers...'

Q (February 2007).

'Buy as many U2 albums as you can afford and the world will be a better place.'

The deceased Jim Morrison, in a message passed on to Bono (or so he says), and declared from the stage at Palais des Omnisports de Bercy, Paris, 7 May 1992, in Mark Chatterton, *The Complete U2 Encyclopaedia* (2001).

'This is quite strange, actually. The only person without his top off is The Edge – everybody else has their clothes off in the studio, and in fact Edge has nothing on from the waist down. Look at Edge's bum! What a bum!'

Dave Fanning, Irish radio presenter, hardly able to contain his excitement during a naked interview, live on RTE's 2FM (25 June 1987).

'Different people have differing abilities to get across the drama, the tension, the percussive qualities of the word 'fuck'.'

Bono, on his mate Bob Geldof, *NME* (April 2006).

'We're not particularly into hit singles. Mind you, I need to do the roof of my house in the West so if we get a few hits away I won't be complaining.'

Edge, *Propaganda* (1991).

'Michael Jackson apparently became obsessed with U2 after *The Joshua Tree* beat *Bad* to Album of the Year at the Grammys, and asked the group if he could send a camera crew to film them working in the studio for his own personal use. Slightly creeped out, U2 refused.'

Q (August 2006).

In March 2003, Bono arranged to have his trilby hat flown from London to Italy for a charity show with Luciano Pavarotti. £100 was paid to deliver the hat from West London to Gatwick airport, where it was placed on a flight to Bologna (£442), and then from Bologna airport to Modena (£150 taxi fare). In what is possibly a first for hat travel, the trilby was removed from business class to the cockpit when it was feared it would be crushed during the flight.

Q (2006).

'Men should not be forced to wear pants when it's not cold.'

Adam Clayton, on his nude appearance on the sleeve of *Achtung Baby*, *Mojo* (November 2006).

'People are interested in bridges. I guess I've always been more interested in what goes on beneath bridges.'

Bono, *Rolling Stone* (14 March 1985).

'U2 Airline is for the Business Class traveller who doesn't give a shit about meetings, business or even where they're going. There's no Economy on *Vertigo 3*, a converted Air Canada Airbus, only maximum leg room high roller class. You can smoke. No one asks you to do up a seat belt. The captain never gets on the mic and tells you the weather at your destination. U2 hostesses who look like characters from *Abigail's Party* – heels, cherry-red chiffon – bring wine and ice lollies and are gentle, chatty and kind.'

Q (January 2006).

'I want you to put El Salvador through your amplifier...'

Bono to Edge, following his visit to Central America in 1986, in Dave Bowler & Bryan Dray, *U2: A Conspiracy of Hope* (1993).

Bono once paid £35,000 for the outfit worn by Charlie Chaplin in the film *The Great Dictator* at an auction in Sotheby's London. It was put on a Charlie Chaplin figure on display at Mr Pussy's De Luxe Café in Dublin.

Mark Chatterton, *The Complete U2 Encyclopaedia* (2001).

'At one show, Paul McGuinness asks the club owner to pay the band in cash. The club owner pulls a gun, insisting that U2 accept payment by cheque, just like everybody else.'

Pimm Jal de la Parra, *U2 Live – a Concert Documentary*, talking about a gig at The Rox venue, Lubbock, Texas, 30 March 1981 (1994).

'If you really hate me or U2 don't shoot me – that will only sell another 5 million records... I'm worth more dead than alive! If you really hate me, don't make me a legend!'

Bono, *Hot Press* (December 1988).

'The members of the band all grab pieces of paper and make lists of what they'd like to see happen to Edge in a chair.

Edge's list is full of suggestions like, "Beautiful women kiss Edge." The guitarist is taken aback when his band-mates' ideas are read out: "Edge gets punched in face", "Cigarette pushed up Edge's nose", "Break egg on Edge's head."'

Edge, getting nervous prior to the shooting of the video for 'Numb', in Bill Flanagan, *U2 at the End of the World* (1995).

'No. But no one's invincible, y'know.'

Larry Mullen Jr, asked if U2 could handle a line-up change, *Q* (March 1997).

Fame and Success

In these days of fake, easily obtained celebrityhood, fame and success don't necessarily go hand in hand. What is either, anyway? A YouTube download? A television series called *Jade's PA*? Most of us will never experience or understand the level of awareness the world has of U2 and, in particular, of Bono. What he and U2 do with their fame and success is down to personal tastes and requirements; you'd have to agree (money aside, with which they can do what they want or like — it's none of our business, is it?) that fame more or less suits U2. They wear it well and without creases. You never see them roll out of a club and become involved in punch-ups because they're too busy being civilised and raising families. Adam Clayton used to be the one who flagrantly abused his position, but now he's sober, he wisely spends his time watering his begonias, buying art and wearing expensive pairs of socks. And why ever not?

'We never had hit singles and now we are described as the band who was so smart they didn't have hit singles — they made albums and they had hit albums. I think the truth is somewhere between the two. We were never prepared to stake our lives on whether or not we could have a hit single.'

Paul McGuinness, *Hot Press Yearbook* (1986).

'I don't think U2 have done anything like their best work yet. I think they're just starting. That sounds odd, but I don't think the band would disagree ... The success, if you want to call it success, that we've enjoyed so far has really only prepared us for being in the position from which we will do what has to be done now.'

Paul McGuinness, *Hot Press Yearbook* (1986).

'If you realise that this friction makes you smarter, quicker and tougher, then it's surely wise to stick with it. But if you want an easy life, if you're happy with your lot, if you see success as your goal, it's over. I've had this out with various members of the band ... Ali ... and we thought, okay, maybe it'll take ten years to get to this place, but when we got there we could stop this kind of madness. But I don't think it's mad. I think that's the fun of it. I think there's nothing sadder than people who feel that they've arrived.'

Bono, in Bill Flanagan, *U2 at the End of the World* (1995).

'Rock's Hottest Ticket.'

Cover strapline, *Time* magazine (27 April 1987).

'We worked to move forward all the time. We always felt we were on a blank canvas and we could go anywhere because we were not trying to imitate anyone else. We were developing our own thing and, for me, that was the image that stood out more than anything else: a band totally driven, very focused, constantly striving to get to what we thought would be the next level, which was always further and further away. In the context of the band, 'no', as in 'it can't be done', is a word that doesn't exist.'

Joe O'Herlihy, U2 audio director, in Diana Scrimgeour, *U2 Show* (2004).

'Last year was the year in which U2 became extraordinarily successful. Success like that does not please everyone. U2 were not the first band to discover that their original small audience contained some people who bitterly resented and resisted their growing popularity around the world.'

Paul McGuinness, giving the keynote address at New York's 9th New Music Seminar, as reproduced in *Hot Press* (11 August 1988).

'There's nothing like being at number one, there really isn't. We had a number one in England [with the album *War*] and we were off to America. There's no feeling quite like it in the world. Everything terrible that ever happened to you in your life was no longer terrible in that moment.'

Bono, in *U2 By U2* (2006).

'I find that hilarious, it's a joke.'

Adam Clayton, on U2 being called the number one rock band in the world, *Hot Press* (October 1988).

'Live Aid, especially, had a huge unanticipated impact on the band, commercially speaking ... [It] was huge, high-profile, international, a once-in-a-lifetime kind of event. And although that wasn't their motivation, it ended up being hugely beneficial to their career. It also ratcheted up the pressure. It was a big turning point. The stakes suddenly got even bigger. It had always been very much a team effort, but what we saw over time is that you can't maintain that small personal family feeling when you've got over 200 people on the road. It's gone.'

Ellen Darst, Principle Management employee from 1983-93, in Diana Scrimgeour, *U2 Show* (2004).

'When I was thirteen I had a vision of myself standing in front of thousands of people. I wasn't even sure I was going to be in a group, I thought I might be a politician or something, but I knew one day I was going to be standing in front of many thousands of people. I have seen this vision come truer and truer.'

Bono, *Sounds* (October 1980).

'I'm famous because I know Bono. That's pretty much it.'

Adam Clayton, *Q* (July 2001).

'One thing that U2 were not precious about that has been the death of so many bands – from The Clash to Nirvana to Lauryn Hill – is that U2 wanted to talk to everyone who would listen. That's the motivation of rock and roll ... It's about appealing to the nerds and to the football players as well as to the people who wore all the right clothes. U2 didn't have that Hamlet complex that at key moments caused people from Sinead O'Connor to Eddie Vedder to doubt the worth of what they were doing. Or to look into the audience and say, "I don't like that person." And that's one of the reasons that U2 have been so successful for so long.'

Bill Flanagan, MTV Networks International and author of *U2 at the End of the World*, in Diana Scrimgeour, *U2 Show* (2004).

'Success is not heavy, it's weightless. Without gravity you're just left to spin.'

Bono, in *U2 By U2* (2006).

'This year's been a dangerous year for U2 in some ways. We're now a household name, like Skippy Peanut Butter or Baileys Irish Cream, and I suppose that makes us public property in a way we weren't before. We've seen the beginning of the U2 myth, and that can become difficult ... For instance, Bono's personality is now so caricatured that I worry whether he'll be allowed to develop as a lyricist the way I know he can.'

Edge, *Rolling Stone* (10 March 1988).

'Success to me was not having to carry or set up my own drums any more.'

Larry Mullen Jr, in *U2 By U2* (2006).

'I think we lost our humour a bit, I really do. It was the bends, really. It was just changing pressure, moving from Dublin suburbia to travelling around the world and all that comes with it.'

Bono on Bono (2005).

'I like to be able to talk to people. I like to be able to spend time with people. I don't like it when they see me as anything other than a person. When people start relating to me as some sort of pop star, I get real freaked out.'

Bono, in a radio interview on Boston's WBCN (November 1984).

'You can only exist at this level through faith, blind ambition or the need for revenge. Or all three. We've had moments of great songwriting, great lyrics. There is no point if you are not trying to better your last album. We're trying. We want to make an album that flows from start to finish, pays off musically, emotionally, lyrically. It has to have at least four singles that make it on Top 40 radio. We want it all and we want it sometime in the next five years!'

Larry Mullen Jr, in *U2 By U2* (2006).

'I'm bored stiff with the quantity of trivia that's been written about the band. I mean, it's fantastic, it's great that we get that much recognition, but I don't know how people stick it, to be honest.'

Edge, talking about publicity, *Dave Fanning Show* on Ireland's 2FM (25 June 1987).

'There was an instance of an edit that both Edge and Bono needed to hear. There was a show, and as soon as it was over Bono was boarding a plane and Edge was going off to do press. As Bono was walking off the stage they handed him a phone, I played him the edit, then called the dressing room, and, because they weren't going to see each other that night, briefed Edge on Bono's input, then got Edge's thoughts, and that's how we finished the song. People think a rock star's life is all glamour and parties, not with this band.'

Cheryl Engels, recording quality controller, in Diana Scrimgeour, *U2 Show* (2004).

'I almost felt being on the ZooTV tour [in 1992] was selling out. I hardly knew U2's music at all. I'm talking to the guitar player a whole bunch of times, and then finally someone from their crew comes up and says, "Hey Michael – you know the guitar player? His name is Edge. Not Ed."'

Michael Franti, musician, *The Irish Times* (July 2006).

Interviewer: 'When did you last wash the dishes or hoover?'

Adam: 'I'd say in the mid-seventies.'

Adam Clayton, *ZooTV Tour Programme* (1992).

'If I can say this without sounding like an asshole, it's the price you pay, unfortunately.'

Larry Mullen Jr, on celebrity, *Dave Fanning Show* on Ireland's 2FM (25 June 1987).

'Nothing was ever impossible to them or to any of us around the band. I think we all felt, from the very early days, that if we were going to do something then it had to be done right. It was as simple as that. People may have demurred, or people may have hiccupped, or people may have blinked, but at the end of the day whatever we set about doing was going to be done. Simple as that. Had to happen.'

Jake Kennedy, U2 director PopMart, in Diana Scrimgeour, *U2 Show* (2004).

'*Rattle And Hum* is perceived as one of U2's failures. We sold 12 million copies of the record, so that is the kind of failure I can live with.'

Paul McGuinness, in *U2 By U2* (2006).

'With Live Aid, what [Paul] McGuinness actually ended up doing was ensuring that U2 got a slot in the UK which was the first slot in America when America came on live. So U2 were the first band seen on Live Aid, in America. That's the type of thing that Paul did that ... probably isn't necessarily appreciated as being what I would consider to be one of the pivotal moments of their career.'

Tim Parsons, UK-based concert promoter, in Diana Scrimgeour, *U2 Show* (2004).

'I don't like this sort of new fan. There used to be a time where there were more fans crashing on the floors of our rooms than standing outside the hotel! Now you get these super-rich groupies staying in bigger suites than the band ... These kind of rich girls, they've got nothing to do with rock 'n' roll. This is celebrity. It's getting harder and harder to meet the people who actually listen to the records.'

Bono, in B.P. Fallon, *U2 Faraway So Close* (1994).

'The shocking thing is that well before we had a right to, we had this belief that we would become a very successful band. From the beginning, Adam never doubted that we would make it big.'

Edge, *Q* (December 1998).

'We were criticised by some people for not revealing more [in the movie *Rattle And Hum*]. We actually made quite a conscious decision not to reveal more because we didn't feel comfortable with it. It is a balance because you have to give up so much more when you reveal all. It's like you no longer have a private life. But at the same time, if you don't reveal all, people don't really get the full picture. So it's a compromise ... My attitude was, "What? Do you think we're crazy? Cameras in the dressing room? What do you think we are – stupid?" ... If it was done in a way where our private lives were an open book, I don't think I could be in the band. I didn't get into the band to become a celebrity. I got into the band because I wanted to play music and write songs and tour ... Some people might object to that but I say, "Well, fuck you!"'

Edge, in Bill Flanagan, *U2 at the End of the World* (1995).

'I don't want people to climb up on a cross and die aged thirty-three to be a great musician. My heroes are survivors, the ones that lived ... I love these people. I'm much more interested in them than in some new star or starlet.'

Bono on Bono (2005).

'Working with U2 was quite different to working with any other outfit. Normally, you don't really get to talk to the artist that often. You get a brief from the record company or video commissioner saying the kind of thing they're after ... But U2 are in control of everything.'

Kevin Godley, film director/contributor to ZooTV, in Diana Scrimgeour, *U2 Show* (2004).

'Celebrity is ridiculous. It's silly, but it is a kind of currency, and you have to spend it wisely.'

Bono on Bono (2005).

'I don't think anyone thinks this is a job for me. I don't think it's healthy to imagine it's always going to be here. I always say two crap albums in a row and we're out. That, and a fat arse, can close this operation down. The price of admission is a level of commitment, and that might get harder and harder for some people, or even myself. We just may not want to go to the gym, they just may not want to have somebody else criticise their work. It gets harder. After you go home, you return to be lords of your own domain. That is the way of males, in particular. They rid the room of argument until they've no one left except people who agree with them. It is understandable, but I like an argument.'

Bono, in *U2 By U2* (2006).

'I'm still not used to hanging out with U2, and I still learn so much from watching them play. Did Bono slip me any answers? No, I'm still waiting on the Bono talk. I don't think we're getting it. He's scared to give it to us! Could you imagine how good we'd be if we had it? It wouldn't be fair!'

Brandon Flowers, lead singer with The Killers, on 'the Bono talk', *NME* (May 2006).

'When we released our first album, even the most moderate success was something to get really excited about. Twenty-five years later, I still get excited but I also feel a huge sense of humility. This really shouldn't be happening. I would have been happy just to have had a record deal at this point.'

Adam Clayton, on the acclaim for *How To Dismantle An Atomic Bomb*, in *U2 By U2* (2006).

'The night I talked to Bono for the first time – when they opened for J Geils at the San Francisco Civic in spring 1981 – he said to me, "I have the vision, I have the energy, I have the commitment. We're going to be the biggest band in the world." I was like, "Oh, my God…" I mean, this was just some opening act. If anyone had said it, you'd just go, "Get the fuck out of here."'

Gregg Perloff, US-based concert promoter, in Diana Scrimgeour, *U2 Show* (2004).

'In a way, we were surprised, but at the same time you don't get involved in a business like this unless you really believe that what you've got to say is worthwhile. We didn't enter into it in a naïve way. We were well aware of the stakes ... Though we've never gone through that period of 'paying our dues' for ten years, we were perfectly prepared to do that if it was necessary, because we believed in what we were doing.'

Adam Clayton, *The New Paper* (17 November 1981).

'We were the only band who played on *Top of the Pops* whose single ['Fire'] went down the chart the next week.'

Edge, on 'Fire' which was released in August 1981, in *U2 By U2* (2006).

'Fame is an obscenity. It's been my experience that the people who give out the most about fame are the people who think the most about it, the people who believe in it.'

Bono, *Q* (February 2002).

'U2 smelt rich ... A pleasing odour.'

Kaiser Chiefs, on their support slot with U2, *Q* (April 2006).

'They know what emotion sounds like. That's the trick to any kind of greatness: you've got to know what it sounds like. It can't be blurred by money or houses or new girlfriends or anything. U2 manage to keep all of that out of the mix. The more people express what they feel through music, rather than thinking about what they should write, just writing it naturally, the more success they will have.'

Jimmy Iovine, chairman of Interscope Records, in Diana Scrimgeour, *U2 Show* (2004).

'I'm generally in awe of it that four people who really didn't know their arse from their elbows and were wet behind their ears can actually travel the world and meet people.'

Adam Clayton, on the band's success, *ZooTV Tour Programme* (1992).

'We always had the grasp, it was just the reach was the problem. It's like a boxer with about six inches missing off his right hook, that's what it felt like in U2 most of the time. Just occasionally, just because we were quick, our inner force would knock one of our goals out, but normally the reach was less than the grasp.'

Bono on Bono (2005).

'From my perspective, everything was going along really nicely, we were making progress by degrees ... Suddenly, *The Joshua Tree* was number one in America, for nine weeks. Then 'Without Or Without You' went to number one. We were on the cover of *Time* magazine. We were no longer trying to conquer America. One moment you are on one side of the fence, the next moment you are catapulted to the other. This was something most bands only dream about; we were the band.'

Larry Mullen Jr, in *U2 By U2* (2006).

'Like most of the rock bands who have had long, successful careers, U2 built their audience one city at a time through their live shows. They came back to America and worked and worked and worked and worked. They toured here so many times between 1980 and 1984 people in Boston thought they were a local band! I think they always saw touring as an essential part of the job, which is another thing that distinguishes them from a lot of people who came along during the 1980s. Other bands figured, "The video is doing the job, the record's doing the job, the photo shoot's doing the job, therefore I don't have to play to 300 people in Boise on a Tuesday night." Whereas U2 said, "Three hundred people in Boise, let's go!"'

Bill Flanagan, MTV Networks International and author of *U2 at the End of the World*, in Diana Scrimgeour, *U2 Show* (2004).

'We really feel that we have nothing to fall back on and we worry about that rock music principle, which is 'two bad albums and you're out'. There is no comfort zone for us. It's all about the incline and decline for us.'

Bono, *Cara* (June 2005).

'I think not having a family and kids, I know what I need. It's not very much actually, which is a nice place to be. Part of it's just opening your eyes and realising that there are practical ways that people live and that's okay. There's nothing wrong with catching the subway in New York – you don't have to get a stretch limo.'

Adam Clayton, *Q* (July 2001).

'I quite enjoy being lost in Africa, wandering around, where people have no idea who I am, but even when they do hear that you're some sort of rich rock star, it doesn't really change they way they talk to me.'

Bono on Bono (2005).

'You know, we're very competitive: we want to be on the radio, have big singles. We don't want to be thought of as a veteran band. We like the fact that people mention Coldplay as our contemporaries.'

Larry Mullen Jr, *Sunday Times Magazine* (7 November 2004).

'Larry's always been noticed cause he's the pretty one. He's honed that character down in a way that he can feel comfortable in public as he didn't used to. And that's enough. His very silence speaks louder than anything else.'

Adam Clayton, in Bill Flanagan, *U2 at the End of the World* (1995).

'I see the embarrassment, excruciating at times, of 'rich rock star works on behalf of the poorest and most vulnerable'. I mean, it's a very embarrassing photograph. Yet you can't deny who you are. And if I gave all my money away, I'd just be a bigger star. Right?'

Bono on Bono (2005).

'It's never about competing with other bands. We compete with ourselves, with the idea of not becoming crap like everyone else does. Because the only way you can justify living like this – with your fancy houses and no money problems – is surely not to be crap.'

Bono, *Q* (November 2004).

'The horse had bolted. I personally apologised on the website. There are ways of managing these things; however, you can never guarantee your audience won't get ripped off by scalpers. U2.com learned some hard lessons, and so have I. Had the militant fans been a little bit more understanding, it might have been easier to navigate our way through the problems. In fairness, though, they had no idea of the reasons why things fell apart. However, it makes you wonder why some people are fans of the group at all, if they think we would deliberately try and exploit them.'

Larry Mullen Jr, on the 'meltdown' of U2.com, brought about by the website unadvisedly guaranteeing tickets for the Vertigo tour, in *U2 By U2* (2006).

'How many bands can do this? U2 and Oasis are the underground and everybody else is the mainstream. Cause they're all afraid to be big. They're afraid of success!'

Noel Gallagher, Oasis linchpin, *Propaganda* (1997).

'I didn't recognise myself in the person I was supposed to be, as far as you could see in the media. There's a kind of rape that happens when you're in the spotlight and you accept it.'

Bono, *Rolling Stone* (4 March 1993).

'Builders and plumbers.'

Larry Mullen Jr, when asked who most of his friends are, *Q* (November 2004).

'We have become the group that we always wanted to become. That in itself inevitably brings you to yet another border in your life and I suppose it means that we really are free to let our imaginations run wild in terms of what we could be now. We've got to the point where we may well be the greatest group in the world. Now what do you do with it?'

Adam Clayton, in Bill Flanagan, *U2 at the End of the World* (1995).

'You think that because you're good at acting, at writing songs, at whatever, that you are somehow a more important person than somebody who, say, is a nurse, or a doctor or a fireman. This is simply not true. And in God's order of things, people like me are very spoiled. I still find it confounding that the world turns people like rock stars or movie stars, artists of any kind, into heroes.'

Bono on Bono (2005).

'That's the bass player's house?!'

Neil Young, in a reported comment on seeing Adam Clayton's twenty-acre estate in Rathfarnham, Dublin, in Bill Flanagan, *U2 at the End of the World* (1995).

'If there was a city that was resisting we would revisit them and do things to make them topple.'

Paul McGuinness, on U2's prolonged touring campaign throughout the 1980s, *Q* (August 2006).

'The people who really revere the cult of celebrity are the ones who spend all their energy trying to avoid it ... No one is a star by accident. To reach that place and cry foul is churlish. The ones that hide do that so they can be discovered. They give it too much energy.'

Bono on Bono (2005).

'We went backstage and talked to him for an hour. There were people hammering on the door saying, "Mr Sinatra, Gregory Peck is here to see you", and Frank was like, "Hold on, I'm with my friends here." Then as we were leaving, he was like, "You wanna racehorse named after you?"'

Edge, on meeting Ol' Blue Eyes backstage in Las Vegas in 1987, *Q* (August 2006).

'It's much easier to be successful than it is to be relevant. The tricks won't keep you relevant. Tricks might keep you popular for a while, but in all honesty, I don't know how U2 will stay relevant. I know we've got a future. I know we can fill stadiums. And yet, with every record, I think, is this it? Are we still relevant?'

Bono, appearing on *The Oprah Winfrey Show* (2004).

'There is the assumption, just because U2 have been successful, that everybody else who is making records is on the same road – and they're not. I think most people out there, they don't have much of an idea of how we've done what we've done. And why it is the way it is. They just see the effects of it.'

Adam Clayton, in John Waters, *Race of Angels – the Genesis of U2* (1994).

'Success has many fathers, but in U2 there's only one father – Paul McGuinness!'

Chris Blackwell, of Island Records, on awarding U2's manager the Peter Grant Award for Lifetime Achievement in Music (May 2006).

'You take fame a little bit seriously by pretending that you didn't want it and that it's an intrusion and that it won't change you. They're all lies. We did want it. It doesn't have to be an intrusion. And it should change you. Why would you want to stay the same?'

Bono, in *U2 By U2* (2006).

'It's a terrible thing to get something before you desire it. We've been lucky. We've generally desired something just before we got it. But then, it's also a mind-fuck to get everything you want.'

Bono, in Bill Flanagan, *U2 at the End of the World* (1995).

'We're not going to surrender to anyone else.'

Paul McGuinness, *Propaganda* (1987).

'When you've sold a lot of records, it's very easy to be megalomaniac enough to believe that you can change things.'

Bono on Bono (2005).

'I understand the power of having a famous face, and I'm not being disingenuous about a certain celebrity status that I might have – it comes in handy here and there, and it's an annoyance here and there. But I'm not sure I'm very good at it.'

Bono, *Vanity Fair* (November 2004).

'The good thing about U2 is it's always been a bit of a struggle. I don't think there was any point where the success was so enormously great that you could completely lose your mind and think you were the Aga Khan ... We didn't have the time or the economic position to experience any grand madness.'

Adam Clayton, *Q* (July 2001).

'It's not important that you might meet 10,000 people. It's important that you meet one person that has something to say to you that's relevant ... I miss being able to meet somebody after a concert and going back to their place and have a coffee or sleep on their floor ... We're getting a bit cut off from that. It's just the way of it and I suppose we have accepted it, reluctantly.'

Bono, *Dave Fanning Show*, on Ireland's 2FM (25 June 1987).

'Everybody receives death threats in a big rock 'n' roll band. We've had them, we'll have them again.'

Bono, *Hot Press* (December 1988).

'We were flying around America and that was great. I wasn't sorry to see the back of the buses. Our plane was like a flying brothel, in terms of décor as opposed to activity.'

Larry Mullen Jr, on the *Joshua Tree* years, in *U2 By U2* (2006).

'I have no illusions at all about myself as to why people care about me. I know why they care about me. I'm in a great band that has stuck together. I'm being open and vulnerable in my music and I've gotten away with it. End of story.'

Bono on Bono (2005).

'Tough work, Edge?'

Larry Mullen Jr, addressing U2's guitarist on his arrival at a German studio to view the shooting of the video for 'Numb' – Edge is sitting on a stool in a black sleeveless T-shirt, with three gorgeous models on the floor around him – in Bill Flanagan, *U2 at the End of the World* (1995).

'They lead – to my mind anyway – a completely artificial life. We were in New York, my older son Norman and his wife and my brother-in-law and his wife, and we were all going out to see *Cats* and Paul was stuck in the hotel and couldn't get out. He said to me, "My God, I'd love to be able to go to a show with you." It's like living in a fishbowl. His life isn't his own. There are obviously tremendous financial advantages, but it's a fairly high price.'

Bob Hewson, on Bono, in Bill Flanagan, *U2 at the End of the World* (1995).

'The moment between the button and the flash. Every phone has a camera now and I really don't mind people taking my photograph but between the button and the flash there can be, like, three hours. That's when the smile that was natural on your face starts to look a little crooked.'

Bono, on what he hates most about being a rock star, *Q* (January 2006).

Witticisms

It has been a criticism of the band from the very start – they have no sense of humour. Perceptually speaking, this was true – for quite a while U2 came across as a perennially dour band, very much into the notion of rock music as a means to deliver a worthy but necessarily dull message. You can blame pretty much everyone connected with the band for this; wilfully, it seems, there was little or no attempt to leaven in the eyes of the public and media the serious nature of what the band did with their output. Image was overlooked in favour of creative import, and it wasn't until after *Rattle And Hum* (which really ground down their attempts at lightening up) and the reinvention of the band as arch ironists that their sense of humour (quite sharp if you look hard enough) took shape.

'It's the line that puts the fear of God in all of us.'
Bono, on Paul McGuinness's infamous eight-word request – 'I have someone I'd like you to meet' – in Bill Flanagan, U2 at the End of the World (1995).

U2 Joke:

Q: How many members of U2 does it take to change a lightbulb?

A: Just one. Bono holds the light bulb and the world revolves around him.

Q (June 1995).

'It's worth a listen to hear his hilarious delivery and fantastic wordplay, including the bit where Ryanair trolley dollies neatly segue into people living and dying on trolleys. It wasn't *Waiting for Godot*, but for most of us it was a darn sight funnier.'

Bernice Harrison, on Bono's homage to Beckett, *The Irish Times* (March 2006).

'Every day, he calls from the Vatican looking for racing tips or greyhound results.'

Christy Moore, on being asked if he talks to Bono, *Mojo* (May 2006).

'Paul is to be congratulated for this sterling effort in arranging the *Blue Peter* appeal for Africa, but he must learn not to get up on stage and insist on doing a 'duet' with the headmaster while he is taking assembly. We also cannot allow him to wear wraparound shades indoors without a letter from his optician.'

Fictitious 'End of Term Report' for Paul Hewson from Mullet Castle Comprehensive School, *Q* (May 2006).

Bono: 'The only song we thought might go to number one was 'One'.

Edge: 'We should have called it 'Fourteen', because that's where it went in the charts.'

Interview with U2, *Propaganda* (1991).

'I'm all for it. Like, why wait until I'm dead? Why not get all that stuff that happens to dead people now? I could come up with a deal. Maybe we could let the tourist buses in.'

Bono, when asked has his birthday become a public holiday in Ireland, in *Bono on Bono* (2005).

Interviewer: 'How come 'Sunday Bloody Sunday' ended up back in the set? Didn't you vow never to play that song again?'

Edge: 'We lied.'

Interview with U2, *Propaganda* (1991).

'After ten years saving the whale, it's like, forget the whale, remember the bank account!'

Larry Mullen Jr, *Vogue* (December 1992).

'Tall, intelligent, modest.'

Bono, on being asked how he was, *Q* (November 2006).

Interviewer: 'What would you like to have that you don't?'

Bono: 'Feet. My legs just seem to end.'

ZooTV Tour Programme (1992).

Wisdom

One person's wisdom is another person's *Reader's Digest* snippet. No one is saying that U2 are more or less 'wise' than the average rock band, but if you believe that U2 are not your average rock band then you'll have to come to the conclusion that, yes, they actually are quite intelligent and that, with the passing of the years and all those books they've read whiling away the hours as they fly in their private jets from gig to home and back again that they've picked up some level of understanding regarding the ways of the world. Yes, Bono can occasionally mistake wisdom for ponderous self-pronouncements, but overall his brain is engaged prior to opening his mouth. Who is the wisest member of U2? Well, not to take away from the others, but we reckon it's undoubtedly Larry — he speaks the least, which means when he does actually say something you know it's probably worth listening to.

'If you're going out for dinner four times a week and you look round the table and everybody's on your payroll, then you've probably become a prick.'

Bono, *Q* (February 2002).

'It comes from the top down. Bono has told me that if any big shot who comes backstage ever gives me a bad time I can tell him to fuck off. Do you know what a relief that is? Some people – LA is the worst for this – are so rude, so demanding and ungrateful. They get complimentary tickets and if they see somebody they know with better complimentary tickets they get upset with us. Their prestige is determined by how good their free seats are!'

Sheila Roche, of Principle Management, in Bill Flanagan, *U2 at the End of the World* (1995).

'From a band with the ethical sense that U2 has had from the beginning, we have a right to hear that they have failed. The market allows them to conceal this. Each year, each record, a new audience discovers them, and is infatuated with the wonder of what they represent(ed). But for those who have been there for a while, never mind the beginning, there is little left but the wonder of their survival and their phenomenality.'

John Waters, *The Irish Book Review* (Autumn/Winter, 2006).

'Your nature is a very hard thing to change; it takes time. One of the extraordinary transferences that happens in your spiritual life is not that your character flaws go away but they start to work for you. A negative becomes a positive: you've a big mouth; you end up a singer. You're insecure; you end up a performer who needs applause. I have heard of people having life-changing, miraculous turnarounds, people set free from addiction after a single prayer, relationships saved where both parties say, "Let go, and let God." But it was not like that for me. For all that "I was lost, I am found" [a line from the U2 song, 'Gloria'], it is probably more accurate to say, "I was really lost, I'm a little less so at the moment." And then a little less and a little less again ... The slow reworking and rebooting of a computer at regular intervals, reading the small print of the service manual. It has slowly rebuilt me in a better image. It has taken years, though, and it is not over yet.'

Bono, in *U2 By U2* (2006).

'I think when you die, you're dead. Next up, Judgment.'

Bono on Bono (2005).

'When people wanna find out the meaning of life just because you can sing in tune, because you can write songs – well, then they got the wrong guy ... People think I've got all the answers when in fact I've just got a whole list of questions.'

Bono, speaking on the DIR Radio Network in America (8 September 1987).

'You should never fight darkness with light, you should just make the light brighter.'

Bono, *Propaganda* (1987).

'You can fall asleep in the comfort of your own freedom. We can't right all the wrongs, but we can find people who can help to do it.'

Bono, *Sounds* (1987).

'Innocence is more powerful than experience. Anton Corbijn did a museum retrospective in Holland, with a room full of Bonos, which was a little disturbing. There was one photo where I saw a face that I don't see any more when I look in the mirror. It's nothing to do with youth – it was a look in the eye and I think it's probably got beaten out of me by the journey. It's the power of innocence.'

Bono, *Q* (July 2001).

'When you're sixteen, you think you can take on the world. And sometimes you're right.'

Bono, *Achtung Baby: the Videos* (1992).

Love

Well, yes, you can feel the love; in fact, it pings off you like a sonar spike. For U2, love doesn't come in spurts, love comes to town. It's another axe to grind for people who don't like the band, yet if we are honest with ourselves (you know, the deep-soul-of-the-night honest), then we would have to admit that love, and only love, makes the world go round. Interestingly, U2's love chart isn't smooth or symmetrical – it's more intrigue and outrage, more shadows and fog than the sweetest thing (although it is that, also). It's like that, we think, because that is what love really is: no fairytale but rather an emotionally rocky path to some kind of personal fulfilment. If we're not honest with ourselves (you know, the wee-small-hours-of-the-morning honest), then, of course, you'll think that love is bollocks, and reckon that 'One' is a great song to play at your wedding. The odds on them staying together? We'll give it eighteen months.

'There have been times in my marriage when I thought about those … nights out, those great girls that showed such promise. Now, with a little experience I think I know what that night would have looked like ... But it's not easy to deal with money, it's not easy to deal with fame, it's not easy to deal with women throwing themselves at you, even being married, perhaps especially being married. No matter how strong you are, no matter how upright, these are real hurdles that you have to figure out how to get over. I will never forget the time Adam saw me in a headlock with some starlet and said to me, "It's fun. It's exciting having sex with someone you don't know ... It's a great adventure getting to know somebody. But as rare as it is to fall in love, it is not as rare as real love, I will die for you love, I will be there when you're sick and when you're frail love. Now that's rare. I would give everything, all these experiences that I'm having, all these different and extraordinary women, I'd give them all up for what you have." I remember Adam telling me that. And if there was one reason for having him as best man at my wedding, that was it, that one conversation.'

Bono, in *U2 By U2* (2006).

'People have tried to figure out our marriage for years. It's simple. Relationships need management and she's a very good manager. There's still a lot I don't know about her. She's a mystery to me. Sometimes, I feel I'm not good enough for her ... I love her.'

Bono, on his wife, Ali, *Q* (November 2004).

'You can't love anyone else without loving yourself. And I guess you probably can't hate anyone else without hating yourself ... Love and mercy – mercy is the outworking of love, but love demands that you try to see things from another person's point of view.'

Bono on Bono (2005).

'There was a heat haze ... and she looked like she was in a pool of water, walking through it. There was something so still about her, and to a person who is not still, it was the most attractive thing in the world.'

Bono, on seeing his future wife, Ali Stewart, in the mid-1970s, in *U2 By U2* (October 2006).

'There is a love between the members of this band that is deeper than whatever comes between us.'

Larry Mullen Jr, in Bill Flanagan, *U2 at the End of the World* (1995).

'About 200 bucks. Didn't even count it. He does it all the time.'

Eric Hausch, Bono's bodyguard on being asked how much money Bono gave a vagrant, *Q* (March 1997).

'I wasn't set up for marriage. I was not the kind of person that any of my friends would say, "He's the marrying kind." But I met the most extraordinary woman and I couldn't let her go ... I'm still in love.'

Bono on Bono (2005).

'I think Bono without Ali would unleash an energy upon the world that might have as much negative effect as it has positive.'

Adam Clayton, in *U2 By U2* (2006).

'Love interrupts, if you like, the consequences of your actions, which in my case is very good news indeed, because I've done a lot of stupid stuff.'

Bono on Bono (2005).

'When I tell people "I go on holidays with Bono" they look at me a little funny, but it has actually worked out really well. We bought it [two houses and land in the South of France] in 1992, it was at least another year before one of the houses was habitable and we spent a lot of time there during 1994. That was our summer of love, as Bono calls it. We had a rare old time.'

Edge, in *U2 By U2* (October 2006).

'Ali still laughs about how, on our honeymoon, I was writing an album called *War*.'

Bono, in *U2 By U2* (2006).

'I met Naomi on a plane when I was seated beside her and couldn't wait to get off the plane to tell Adam, because Adam had harboured a crush on Naomi for years. So I set them up on a date. And the rest, as the fellah said, is not history.'

Bono, in *U2 By U2* (2006).

'I know a lot of homosexual men and most of them I get on with. Some overtly camp men I don't get on with. But it all comes down to love. How can anyone attack love? I could never attack love.'

Bono, *Hot Press* (March 1987).

'Something strange happened towards the end of The Joshua Tree tour. We had campaigned for Martin Luther King Day in Tempe, Arizona, where the tour opened ... We went back to Tempe at the end of the tour ... I was getting death threats throughout the tour. One in particular was taken very seriously by the FBI. This character was a racist offended by our work, he thought we were messing in other people's business and taking sides with the black man. One night the FBI said, "Look, it's quite serious. He says he has a ticket. He said he's armed. And he said if you sing 'Pride (In The Name Of Love)', he's going to shoot you." So we played the show, the FBI were around, everyone was a little unnerved. You just didn't know – could he be in the building? Up in the rafters? On the roof? During 'Pride' ... I was singing the third verse, "Early morning April 4, a shot rings out in a Memphis sky." I just closed my eyes and sang. And when I opened my eyes, Adam was standing in front of me.'

Bono, in *U2 By U2* (October 2006).

'Ten years later, ten years down the road from Two-Tone, the funny haircuts, the miserabalists, the post-modern ironists and the pop schemers, who would have thought that the dreamers hold the balance? Who would have thought that with thousands moving on a new psychedelic groove thang or finding themselves moving in a new orbit of future funk, that in 1989 the most potent rock 'n' roll show on the planet would be one based on a rigorous assertion of those old unfashionable concepts 'love' and 'peace'.'

Gavin Martin, *NME* (16 December 1989).

Disputes

They love each other, so of course they argue, fuss and fight. Sometimes over the smallest of things, like deodorant and the ownership of backstage towels; sometimes over big things, such as songs, music and whether that satellite link to Sarajevo during the ZooTV tour was really such a good idea after all. But then, after tempers have subsided, they kiss and make up. It's a bit like love, really – you can't spend over thirty years in the company of the same people without getting narky with each other now and again. They are one but they're not the same. Isn't that right?

'The Edge and myself left the band for a while, certainly in our heads. But nobody else would have us.'

Bono, on the time around the writing and recording of their second album, *October*, *Hot Press* (December 1988).

'When they told me there wasn't going to be a tour and they were going to stay in Dublin and do God's work, whatever it was, I was really shocked ... I went out ... and walked around the block. I came back and I said, "Look, quite honestly, if

God had something to say about this tour he should have raised his hand a little earlier because, in the meantime, we've booked a big crew and made commitments to people and, in my view, you're obliged to follow through on them." So that was kind of the end of it. They accepted that, and it never happened again.'

Paul McGuinness, talking about early 1981 when *October* was written and recorded, in *U2 By U2* (2006).

'For months [Bono] had been uptight about everything, including the music being played behind him. He'd turn and glare at Larry, Edge or Adam if a drum pattern changed or a guitar deviated from the line ... Towards the end of the gig, Larry's snare stand broke. All Bono knew was that Larry had stopped playing. He forgot about audience and performance and turned, enraged, to find Larry grinning sheepishly. Bono charged, hurling his awkward bulk at the drummer, who took evasive action by jumping off backstage. Bono kicked the drum kit over. As it crashed around the stage the audience roared approval. They thought this was part of the show. Bono ran after Larry. As he got to the rim of the stage, Edge reached out and grabbed him by the hair. The guitarist rarely lost his cool, but now the Welsh passion so slowly roused boiled over and raged at Bono. Edge wanted to kick the singer's head in.'

Description of a gig at Toad's Place, New Haven, Connecticut, 15 November 1981, in Eamon Dunphy, *Unforgettable Fire – the Story of U2* (1987).

'Edge smacked me. It was actually a full-on rumble with all members of the band whacking at me and me whacking at them. It was pure pantomime ... But Edge packs a punch.

There's a lesson here: never pick a fight with a man who earns his living from hand to eye co-ordination.'

Bono, recalling the New Haven incident, in *U2 By U2* (2006).

'Bono could be unpredictable, back then he was always ready for a scrap. He was a terrier and had no fear, you always had that in the back of your mind. No matter how upset you became with him, the only way to deal with it was to run for your life.'

Larry Mullen Jr, recalling the New Haven incident, in *U2 By U2* (2006).

'We don't fight, but we all have very strong personalities. But in the end we want the same thing.'

Larry Mullen Jr, *Sunday Times Magazine* (7 November 2004).

'I wouldn't underestimate the level of rage beneath those sweet notes that Edge plays. He can throw a dig. He nearly knocked me out one night.'

Bono on Bono (2005).

'It is by far the most considerate operation of its size I have ever seen in the rock world. The sort of backstabbing and dirty fighting that is routine in most comparable outfits is almost absent ... Even the tensions and fights tend to be like arguments in a family.'

Bill Flanagan, *U2 at the End of the World* (1995).

'I thought this might be the end. We had been through tough circumstances before and found our way out, but it was always outside influences that we were fighting against. For the first time ever, it felt that cracks were within. And that was a much more difficult situation to negotiate.'

Larry Mullen Jr, on the difficult recording process surrounding *Achtung Baby*, in *U2 By U2* (2006).

'We are as good at keeping out of each other's way as we are at being together.'

Paul McGuinness, *Irish Times Magazine* (25 August 2001).

'The sort of criticism we got over Mother [U2-instigated, Dublin-based record label] from younger bands who wanted to put us in the clichéd role of being Led Zeppelin and therefore casting themselves as The Clash and The Sex Pistols, without having a thimbleful of the talent that those two groups have ... I realised that it was something I could do without.'

Bono, *Hot Press* (December 1988).

The real problem in a relationship is when the arguing stops.'
Bono on Bono (2005).

'The album didn't sell as well as hoped. "More than anything else, we were unfortunate that we were on Island at the same time as they had U2. Record companies always have to choose one. We were on the same bill at the Clarendon and blew them away." He also reckons Bono copied his speaker-clambering antics and The Edge copied J.R.'s cowboy hat and Flying V combination, plus lead-rhythm-and-reverb guitar style. "They just took it from us, man," he sighs, still miffed.'

Dennis Morris, a member of 1980s British band Basement 5, in conversation with Kris Needs, *Mojo* (January 2007).

'We are a tight family, with all the pluses and disadvantages of that. But we don't have an ego problem in the band. We all are involved in the process. We all struggle together.'

Larry Mullen Jr, *Sunday Times Magazine* (7 November 2004).

'I don't think U2 have walked on anybody or kicked anyone in the balls ... We may have kicked each other in the balls a few times, but that's another story.'

Bono, *Propaganda* (1987).

'There is a lot of support for each other and a lot of leeway and a lot of understanding. I like to think it would be difficult for one of us to really get off the wall and really go out there without the others realising it and being there to do something about it.'

Edge, in Bill Flanagan, *U2 at the End of the World* (1995).

'Edge thumped me a while back. It was at a gig, though, not in the studio. If you wanna smack somebody about, when you've known each other as long as us, it's hard. You can hurt a lot more with a cruel, off-the-cuff remark. That'll do more damage.'

Bono, Q (March 1997).

'U2 have had a policy over the years of giving good value ... Our reputation for fair play was so well established that we felt the proposed ticket prices were reasonable ... We felt that people would be interested in paying to see U2 and B.B. King performing together in a comparatively intimate setting ... It seems we have made a mistake. We will therefore be dropping the ticket prices to IR£16 [from IR£20.50] standing and IR£18 [from IR£25.50] seating ... As for the question of whether the shows are for charity or not, I will simply restate U2's long-held policy of never discussing, with the media or other third parties, any charitable or philanthropic contributions we make ... It must now be asked whether this peculiar coalition of priests and other commentators will bring their enormous influence to bear on other more essential pricing issues of the day. Petrol? The cost of travel? Should the agricultural sector be subsidised? What about interest rates? Coal and butter?'

Paul McGuinness, making a statement to *Hot Press* regarding the controversy over ticket prices for U2's Dublin shows in December 1989.

'The classic rock and roll star disease is being surrounded by people who agree with you. It gets harder and harder to work with a bunch of people who are your equals and who don't always agree with you. Especially if you've known them a long time. I see people as they go through life getting rid of arguments, shedding friends, every year, till they're left with just one or two people who agree with them. But I always think you're as good as the arguments you get. I like to be around a row.'

Bono, *Propaganda* (1997).

'If Bono left, we could carry on. If I left, we'd be screwed.'

Larry Mullen Jr, *Mojo* (July 2005).

'Bono was spending more and more time on the phone, talking to world leaders, arranging to meet the Pope. There was some grumbling about the amount of time it was taking up, and Brian [Eno] and Danny [Lanois] were very frustrated. The big question was whether it was having an impact on the band's music? The answer was a resounding no. Was it having an impact on the way the band was functioning outside the music? The answer is yes. But nobody could argue with what he was doing, it was clearly too important. And believe me, if we could have, we would have.'

Larry Mullen Jr, in *U2 By U2* (2006).

'I would be terrified to be on my own as a solo singer, not to have a band to argue with. I mean, I surround myself with argument, and a band, a family of very spunky kids, and a wife who's smarter than anyone.'

Bono on Bono (2005).

'We are not hugely intimate with each other, yet there is tremendous tolerance, room and understanding and love. There is intimacy, but a lot of the time it is a work situation and then everyone goes back to their families. It's more adult ... We are our own survival mechanism.'

Adam Clayton, *Sunday Times Magazine* (7 November 2004).

'Personalities will not break up U2. Musical differences will not break up U2. We'll break up because somebody squeezed the toothpaste from the wrong end.'

Larry Mullen Jr, *U2 By U2* (2006).

'There are four evil motherfuckers in U2. I think we would've broken up years ago if there'd been any pansies in the band.'

Edge, *Q* (November 2002).

'Bono wanted us all to share a place. I told him, I'm happy to come here but I'm not living in the same house as you.'

Larry Mullen Jr, on life for U2 in the South of France, *Q* (November 2004).

'We tend to have [arguments] in a very, very careful way. One of the things about living with the same five people over ten years is that it teaches you to have disagreements very carefully – nobody wants to start discussions by saying "Well, this is my point of view and anyone who wants to disagree with me can fuck off." That would paralyse our operation, so they never start like that.'

Paul McGuinness, *Propaganda* (1987).

'You look at most people in their thirties and forties – and not just the ones in bands – and they've got rid of the people in their life that are friction, that they clash with. That means you're left with nobody to row with, and that to me is no good. That's what keeps you sharp. That's why I'm happy with still being in a band ... I couldn't imagine a future without the four of us.'

Bono on the topic of U2 splitting up, *Q* (February 1998).

'Belonging to a band means shouting abuse at one another constantly. It's like a lovers' quarrel, intense and passionate ... As you get old, why would you want to bother with all the tension and rows that come with being in a band? That's a good question.'

Bono, *Libération* (9 October 2000).

'The people who know us can read between the lines. The people who listen to our records – they're not fooled by it. The fact of the matter is that we went to a lot of trouble to help Sinead's career in the early days. And that's what you do, if you can ... Bono in particular pioneered Sinead. He went to a lot of trouble encouraging her ... Edge used her on the soundtrack for *Captive*; there were various negotiations with Ensign Records [Sinead O'Connor's first record label] that Ossie Kilkenny [then U2 accountant] was involved in – so she's talking crap ... It's stupid. It's immature. She'll learn. But I know damn well that she won't be making records in ten years. I was interested in her because I thought she was a great talent and I thought she had a future. That's why you support people. Now I'm not so sure that she has what it takes to last.'

Adam Clayton, on criticism from Sinead O'Connor, *Hot Press* (October 1988).

'I think the band is in serious danger sometimes. It's not something you can take for granted. I think it is much more likely that people part company than it is that they stay together.'

Bono, on the band splitting up, in *Bono on Bono* (2005).

'I don't know if it's ever been contemplated. Maybe around the second album, *October*, when people decided that maybe this was too hard. And maybe around the time of *Achtung Baby* and the ZooTV tour. That seemed an immense challenge at the time. But I think splitting up is something that we can't imagine.'

Adam Clayton, on the band splitting up, *Q* (November 2000).

'You could say U2 are a democracy. The decision-making process is the same now as when we started. Those with the ability to debate, argue and articulate their views win the day. If you are in a band with someone as talkative, argumentative and persuasive as Bono, well, things can be kind of difficult for the rest of us.'

Larry Mullen Jr, in *U2 By U2* (2006).

U2:
The Case Against

No one says you have to love U2. No one says you have to like what they say, sing, perform, make and do. No one says you have to go along with the oft-held notion that U2 are the Best Rock Band In The World. No one says that you have to agree with Bono's pronouncements on serious social and political issues, on Adam's knowing remarks about organic fruit juices, on Edge's enthusiastic comments about guitar gadgets or on Larry's heroic thoughts on why he dislikes U2 hangers-on. Which is why democracy holds sway, why opinion of every kind counts for something, and why it's sometimes quite refreshing to read someone ripping the arse out of the fabric that can occasionally wrap up the members of U2 like a stuffed turkey and hang them out to dry.

'They redeemed themselves with their last two albums, but I really disliked them in the early days ... I still feel they're not talented enough to take on being The Best Group In The World, even if their sales figures, image and general demeanour lends itself to that title. I mean, who is it between? U2 and Metallica? I prefer Metallica, actually.'

Nick Kent, former *NME* rock writer, *Hot Press* (10 August 1994).

'"Only the little people pay taxes," as Leona Helmsley loftily observed to her maid. Which may explain why U2's publicity machine has been trying so hard for so long to persuade us that Bono is really more than five feet six inches tall.'

Hugh Linehan, *The Irish Times* (August 2006).

'There was some bemusement if not antipathy to U2 among the British rock press because they were able to be a more successful band in Britain staying based in Dublin than many groups on the mainland.'

Gavin Martin, *NME* (16 December 1989).

'Why should multimillionaires be exempt from any tax just because they've made a few hit records? And why now should we take seriously the pronouncements of a man [Bono] who believes we should all cough up more cash – but that he shouldn't?'

Hugh Linehan, *The Irish Times* (August 2006).

'I share Bono's desire to see more resources devoted to Ireland Aid, but it is more difficult to make a case for it if everyone is not willing to be part of the social contract that stipulates that everybody should pay their fair share in what is a low tax country.'

Joan Burton, Labour Party (Ireland) spokeswoman on Finance, *The Irish Times* (August 2006).

'We're filming the [Elevation] tour for the DVD in Boston, we have a row with our fans, right, because there's people on the road who are in the first row every night ... We're saying, can we just play to the people of the town we're in, instead of one that's following us? They organise a sitdown in the heart of the stage front ... I mean, we understand you can make a protest but not while we're filming. So even our audience are rough. Go to U2 internet sites, they're murder.'

Bono, speaking on Ireland's RTÉ 2FM (2005).

'[Words such as] 'Irishness and independence', 'spirituality', 'community' and 'imagination' are always good for a giggle when you wonder just what Bono's lyrics would have been like had it not been for the blokes who wrote the Bible.'

George Byrne, *Irish Independent* (27 May 2006).

'Never liked them. That whole thing of Bono becoming the Pope – what the fuck's that all about? Pseudo-American rubbish.'

Paul Weller, *Daily Mail* (May 2006).

'Fortune, it is clear, favours neither the bravest nor the most extravagantly talented. The smart ones are its darlings and they don't come any cannier than U2.'

Ed Power, *Irish Independent* (17 February 2005).

'You know what irritates me about modern music? It's all based on ego. Look at a group like U2. Bono and his band are so egocentric – the more you jump around, the bigger your hat is, the more people listen to your music. The only important thing is to sell and make money. It's nothing to do with talent. The Beatles had a value which will last forever. Today there are groups who sell lots of records and then disappear. Will we remember U2 in thirty years? I doubt it.'

George Harrison, *BBC News* (15 November 2000).

'I'm used to the custard pies. I've even learnt to like the taste of them.'

Bono, *The Independent* (16 May 2006).

'The most boring band in the world. There may be groups equally as dull, but I fail to see how any of them can be worse.'

David Quantick, *NME* (November 1984).

'*Hot Press* did their annual yearbook in Dublin and in the course of a long interview I was asked about U2 and Mother Records, and with my great honesty I said that basically I despised U2 and the music they made and what they represented. I didn't find this a contradiction but some of them found it a major contradiction. I always thought they had the capacity to accept criticism or accept somebody disliking them or their music.'

Fachtna O'Ceallaigh, former manager of The Boomtown Rats, in Bill Flanagan, *U2 at the End of the World* (1995).

'The reason I despise them and hate them is because of the lies and rubbish they propagate about Ireland and the out-and-out British-supporting propaganda that they put forward around the world. The idea of some major rock star going around the world with a white flag in his hand and singing 'Sunday Bloody Sunday' and then saying, "This is not a rebel song", has some nerve, as far as I'm concerned, to exploit the pain and suffering of people in a part of ... whether its his own country or anybody else's. That's the problem I have with them.'

Fachtna O'Ceallaigh, former manager of The Boomtown Rats, in Bill Flanagan, *U2 at the End of the World* (1995).

'There isn't a band in Dublin who could get anywhere if they aren't in some way associated with U2.'

Sinead O'Connor, in Dave Bowler & Bryan Dray, *U2: A Conspiracy of Hope* (1993).

'Everybody's got their own tastes so I can't expect everyone to like the band. But I'd hope they'd respect our achievement.'

Larry Mullen Jr, *Hot Press* (30 November 1984).

'They could never fool me! We always had to see over and over again on any television channel that shithead climbing up and down the PA at Redrocks! That guy with the bubble butt waving a white flag! ... And Edge doing that fucking fake-ass pilgrim gig like, "I'm so pious and low key with my millions ..." They've been milking that same bassline and the same guitar change for like five albums ... The world kisses their ass and it is the biggest pile of shite I have ever heard.'

Henry Rollins, letting off steam, in Bill Flanagan, *U2 at the End of the World* (1995).

U2:
The Case For

No one says you have to hate U2 either.

'I think Bono's great ... Like Eddie Izzard, he's somebody who's not afraid of the big idea, and launching himself for it. And if it fails, it fails, but the excitement and the thrill is going for it ... I'm very interested in him as a man, and some of the stuff that he does repels me and some of the stuff I find very interesting. But I do like him ... I'd be bewitched by him, maybe ... I fantasise about walking across deserts with people, but I'd love to do that with Bono. More than the other three. What're their names again?'

Tommy Tiernan, *Hot Press* (17 May 2006).

'I think the people slagging off Bono should get over their own jealousy and get off their asses and try to achieve something themselves ... But I believe that the majority of people recognise what he has achieved will support him.

After all, you don't get nominated for the Nobel Peace Prize for nothing.'

Helena Christensen, *Sunday World Magazine* (2006).

'Bono's greatest talent is that he has a nose for a room and an instinct on how to work it. He's so brimming with talent that it's unbelievable.'

Michael Colgan, director of Dublin's Gate Theatre, *Irish Independent* (31 March 2006).

'Some may question [Bono's] sincerity, a few may occasionally question his integrity, plenty will diss his music, but a quarter-century down the line, it's getting harder to find people who really, really, have a problem with U2. They're an institution.'

Derek O'Connor, *Dubliner* (June 2005).

'From Live Aid in 1985 and Amnesty International's 1986 Conspiracy of Hope tour, through to Live 8 [in 2005], U2 has arguably done more than any other band to highlight the cause of global human rights in general and Amnesty International's work in particular. Their leadership in linking music to the struggle for human rights and human dignity worldwide has been groundbreaking and unwavering.'

Irene Khan, Amnesty International's secretary general, awarding U2 the Amnesty International Ambassador of Conscience Award (December 2005).

'Once I met Bono I knew I had to work with him. I thought there was something about him – something that made the idea of spending time in a studio with him very interesting ...

He talked of how they work as a band, not in terms of playing and so forth, but in terms of contribution, what contributed to the identity of the band as a whole. I hadn't heard anyone talking about a band like that in a long time, and on that basis, out of curiosity, I agreed to work with them.'

Brian Eno, *Propaganda* (1986).

Reviews, Critics
and the Media

You don't get to the stage U2 are at now without someone saying something very nice or nasty. It comes with the territory of being in a position of relative power. You'd have to say, though, that U2 take both pot shots and plaudits in their stride; they also engage with the media in a way that most if not all of their contemporaries do not. This could be due to the fact that they seem to thrive on feedback, they like the actual idea of ideas and they find the cut and thrust of debate intellectually stimulating. They also use the media, however, in quite a strategic manner, which means they know what it can and cannot do, what it can enhance and inhibit. They even read their own reviews, and not out of ego but as a form of instruction. And besides, they do most of their interviews from their houses in the South of France. Which is nice.

'Any band that ever depended on the critics is usually broken up by the critics.'
Bono on Bono (2005).

'The media has rock and roll by the balls. They draw cartoons, and it's indelible ink. It's an attempt to reduce you, your humanity, your sense of humour. The only way to deal with it is to create a cartoon even bigger.'

Bono, *Rolling Stone* (1 October 1992).

'It's impossible to take U2 as seriously as they take themselves. When Bono emotes lines like "No one is blinder than he who will not see ..." I want to wish him a speedy recovery from adolescence.'

Review of *October*, *Rolling Stone* (1981).

'U2 are the most important band in the history of popular music – about ten million leagues ahead of anyone else, past or present. Sometimes, it seems like they exist to show just how mediocre everything else has been.'

John Waters, *In Dublin* (25 June 1987).

'The real problem with it is that it starts from the basic concept that U2 are somehow a cultural force rather than a reasonably good rock singles band with a nifty guitarist and an extremely astute manager.'

George Byrne, reviewing Visnja Cogan, *U2 – an Irish Phenomenon*, *Irish Independent* (27 May 2006).

'If hubris has a sound, then this is it.'

The Observer review of the PopMart tour (1997).

'When U2 do come, they do so via a wall of blinking white lights, Edge's unmistakable ringing guitar notes summoning 'City Of Blinding Lights'. Bono appears, clad in black, marching up a runway from the centre of the stadium, hoisting a Stars and Stripes flag above his head. It's a handy summation of all that will follow: dramatic, epic, crowd-pleasing, and fronted by a man who knows neither fear nor shame.'

Review of U2's final concert of their Vertigo tour, Aloha Stadium, Honolulu, Hawaii, 9 December 2006, *Q* (February 2007).

'They are their own toughest critics. Really, no one else counts. In fact, U2 has always been determined not to allow the records, if you like, to dominate their career.'

Paul McGuinness, in Diana Scrimgeour, *U2 Show* (2004).

'If you're talking about music, I think a lot of the people who know most about music are critics. And there are many critics that I have a lot of time for ... I'm certainly not one of those people who say that critics don't matter. Critics keep you sharp, I think.'

Paul McGuinness, *Hot Press* (4 October 2006).

'Please, please U2, will you take a break and let somebody else hog the limelight for a while? We'll be happy to hear your next album in 2008, but a year free of Bono's musings would be really great.'

John Meagher, rock critic, giving his wish for 2007, *Irish Independent* (22 December 2006).

'The criticism wasn't unexpected. We had reached the point where something had to give. Some of the reviews were extremely harsh but that's showbusiness. Criticism is a hard station for anybody and I think you can take it when you do something crap. But while the movie might have been a mistake, it wasn't crap. And I'll stand over those songs any day ... We should have disappeared for a couple of years and reinvented ourselves. But for all of the pain of seeing your work being described as pompous, arrogant and out of touch, it did inspire us to go and chop down *The Joshua Tree*.'

Larry Mullen Jr, on the reception of the *Rattle And Hum* movie and album, in *U2 By U2* (2006).

'Early on, if we were misquoted, or if someone made something up about us, we'd get very pissed off but now you just have to accept that that's what newspapers and journalists are about. Newspapers aren't about telling people what's actually going on, they're about selling papers, they're as commercially minded as any other. They have to be, and sometimes you're the victim of that.'

Edge, *Propaganda* (1987).

'If I wasn't doing what I'm doing now, I'd be doing what you're doing now.'

Bono, on being asked what was the best thing about being editor for a day at *The Independent*, *Q* (January 2007).

'Another example of rock music's impotence and decay.'

Review of *War*, *NME* (March 1983)

'*The Joshua Tree* rescues rock from its decay, bravely and unashamedly basing itself in the mainstream before very cleverly lifting off into several higher dimensions. They've been misunderstood occasionally, even by their committed supporters – but after *The Joshua Tree*, with its skill, and the diversity of issues it touches, one thing is absolutely clear: U2 can no longer be patronised with faint and glib praise. They must be taken very seriously indeed after this revaluation of rock.'

Bill Graham, *Hot Press* (February 1987).

'Remember the one about Maire Ni Bhraonain? First, Adam was supposed to be having an affair with her, then me – in the end we thought we should have a picture taken of all four of us in bed with Maire. That would've confused them.'

Bono, on the media fabricating news stories about U2, *Hot Press* (June 1987).

'It was an interesting book. I think it got a lot of criticism at the time from music journalists – because most of them in Dublin thought they should have written it! But I think at the time it was a very good thing to have somebody from another world, if you like, coming in and seeing what they made of it.'

Paul McGuinness, on Eamon Dunphy's, *The Unforgettable Fire - the Story of U2*, published in 1987, *Hot Press* (4 October 2006).

'U2 are important not because they drive around in stretch limos, or get on the cover of *Time*, or get to play with Bob Dylan, but because of their music. That seems axiomatic, but sometimes you get to wondering if it needs to be said ... The media in recent months has been focusing on the shadow of U2's achievement and not enough on the substance.'

John Waters, *In Dublin* (25 June 1987).

'The catalogue of errors piles up until it is impossible to see beyond it. If what I know firsthand is so inaccurately represented ... then I can have no faith in any of the rest of Dunphy's storytelling. There is simply nothing I can take at face value in this book ... As a biography [it] is shoddy. As a musical biography, it is a travesty. And Dunphy has no one to blame but himself. In his sports writing, he constantly espouses the pursuit of excellence and is caustically contemptuous of anyone who does not meet his 'exacting' standards. Well, it is time to turn that famously abrasive voice upon himself. He may have been a first class footballer, but this is a fourth division book.'

Neil McCormick, reviewing Eamon Dunphy, *The Unforgettable Fire – the Story of U2*, *Hot Press* (3 December 1987).

'In many ways, we intensely regret having done the book because Eamon took us absolutely at our word, and I suppose that we didn't think he would dig as deeply as he would and find out the things that he did ... It is a pity that he reneged on his promise to let us correct errors. I suppose he was pressurised by his publisher ...'

Paul McGuinness, *Propaganda* (1987).

'He's a curious front man, this young man named Paul Hewson. He looks like a chubby Ron Wood...'

Minneapolis Star and Tribune (May 1983).

'What can I say? That U2 were an experience that defies the written word? We were overwhelmed by their music and lifted by their feeling, and the world outside seemed a million miles away as we were carried into a land of passion and beauty.'

Karen Swayne, *Sounds* reviewer, getting carried away (December 1981).

'*The Joshua Tree* finally confirms on record what this band has been slowly asserting for three years now on stage: U2 is what the Rolling Stones ceased being years ago – the greatest rock 'n' roll band in the world.'

Review of *The Joshua Tree, Los Angeles Times* (1987).

'I'll walk into the pub and some old guy will go, "Larry, yer man Bono, he's a fucking eejit."'

Larry Mullen Jr, on being accosted by strangers in Dublin, *Q* (November 2004).

'The Faustian pact *Musician* editor Flanagan made for such extensive access seems to have resulted in a certain self-censorship: there's nothing here any member of U2 will blush about in the way of petulance, drugs or extra-curricular sex.'

Review of Bill Flanagan, *U2 at the End of the World, Q* (June 1995).

'I just wonder why they don't want us to win? I feel it's an old public school thing. We're the outsiders being dragged through the bushes. We're the ruddy Irish boys getting a kicking.'

Bono, on the adverse UK press on the PopMart tour, *Propaganda* (1997).

'*The Unforgettable Fire* is a story of a rock 'n' roll band written by someone who refers to the phrase "be bop a lu la" as "be bop a loo loo". Dunphy's lack of understanding of rock 'n' roll, his apparent lack of interest in it, his possible dislike for it, leads him inexorably to a vision of U2 as being entirely separate from the rest of popular music culture. It is an assumption which is as stupidly wrongheaded and sloppy as it will be misleading for those who come to the book wondering what it is that distinguishes U2 and makes them great.'

Neil McCormick, reviewing Eamon Dunphy, *Unforgettable Fire - the Story of U2, Hot Press* (3 December 1987).

'*The Joshua Tree* is as close to a perfect statement of where rock 'n' roll is at after over thirty years as anyone could wish to send to their relatives on Mars. It is a sign of hope, of redemption, in the barren desert which rock music has become: U2 have assimilated, refined, filtered the language of rock and distilled it into a piece of crystal.'

John Waters, *In Dublin* (25 June 1987).

'I can't believe U2 are still winning awards. They're crap and boring. And their recent tax exile shows that they obviously don't believe in charity starting at home.'

Alan McArthur, co-author of *Is It Me Or Is Everything Shit?*, *Irish Mail on Sunday* (26 November 2006).

'*Rattle And Hum* is populist, a stance highly unfashionable among those who fastidiously despair of popular culture, who, in their secret treason see the only useful remaining creative activity as the preserve of those marginalised dandies of the soul who refine emotions and experiences untranslatable to the public arena.'

Bill Graham, reviewing *Rattle And Hum, Hot Press* (20 October 1988).

'Some of the recent pieces on us have concentrated perhaps too much on the U2 phenomenon ... and forgotten above all we're a rock band. The music is articulate in a way that I'm

not. I'm almost a liability to the group because I'm so open
– I haven't yet learnt how to hold the cards close to my
chest.'

Bono, *Time Out* (20 May 1987).

'People will be coming up to me thinking, "You're an idiot",
but then they'll come back up to you, as each day progresses
towards the midnight launch, and they shake your hand and
say, "We don't agree with your music, we think U2 are a pile
of crap, but we have to admire the fact that you've stood
here."'

Martin Shanahan, a Cork man who has been travelling from
London to Dublin for more than fifteen years for his chance
to be the first owner of the latest U2 album, *The Irish Times*
(17 November 2006).

'It would be rather cynical of us to suggest that this, U2's
third 'Best Of' in under ten years, was cobbled together to
make some filthy lucre from the Christmas market. Cynical
that is, but quite possible ... Largely unnecessary.'

Review of *U218 Singles*, *NME* (25 November 2006).

'This is clearly the sound of U2's own private jukebox. When
other acts' record companies seem to dash off these
collections in their sleep, there's a sense of personal care and
attention here, as if the whole thing comes with U2's
personal seal of approval. What do you know? It seems we've
been touched again.'

Review of *U218 Singles*, *Q* (January 2007).

'U2's true contribution to Irish life since 1980 has been
largely to do with intangibles such as attitude, self-

confidence and atmosphere. It started off in a country where failure was endemic; they soundtracked the emergence of a country where success came to be worshipped. Perhaps the band's greatest achievement has been to encourage people to consider the relationship between these two countries, these Irelands of the mind – what was left behind when the old Ireland was jettisoned, and what was gained (and lost) when the new Ireland was embraced.'

Gerry Smyth, *Noisy Island – a Short History of Irish Popular Music* (2005).

'Bullshit. Absolute bullshit.'

Adam Clayton, on the news that he was to marry supermodel Naomi Campbell, in Bill Flanagan, *U2 at the End of the World* (1995).

'But I'm reading it everywhere.'

Paul McGuinness, on the news that Adam Clayton was to marry supermodel Naomi Campbell, in Bill Flanagan, *U2 at the End of the World* (1995).

'You're probably telling them.'

Adam Clayton, responding to Paul McGuinness, in Bill Flanagan, *U2 at the End of the World* (1995).

'I hate it. It's like pulling teeth ...'

Bono, on reminiscing on U2's career for the book *U2 By U2*, *Sunday Independent* (24 September 2006).

'The strongest sense from this book is that it takes us nowhere new. It has much in it that is interesting, challenging, moving and important, but, when you have finished flicking through it, looking at the pictures and reading quotes here and there, you are left with the sense that it represents merely the raw research for some further assessment and analysis.'

John Waters, reviewing *U2 By U2*, *The Irish Book Review* (Autumn/Winter, 2006).

'Forget the other groups. Remember U2.'

Review of U2's gig at the Bayou Club, Washington DC, *The Washington Post* (4 March, 1981).

The Ego Has Landed

You don't make omelettes without breaking eggs, and you don't become one of the world's biggest and most successful rock bands without having some kind of idea about levels of self-worth, self-belief and self-promotion. It's a different matter entirely if someone doesn't have the necessary skills, talent and creative wherewithal to back up claims of greatness. It's perhaps not too unreasonable to say that out of U2 it is Bono who has the largest ego. He has, however, also the biggest responsibility towards the band in making them seem (visually, at least, on stage and on film) larger than life itself. So the ego lands – and, it seems, always on its feet.

'I must say I prefer playing Wembley Arena, I really do, that is no joke. The music never seemed to fit into those places. They always seemed too small ... We wanted to blow the roof off. I always felt like that. We needed to find a bigger place to play even if there weren't any people there.'

Bono, when asked did he have a hankering to play small Dublin music venue McGonagle's again, *Propaganda* (1988).

'Yes, I did ... I knew it would be this big.'

Paul McGuinness, on being asked had he ever envisaged U2's success, *Propaganda* (1987).

'If I'm working on a guitar part that's somehow not as good as it could be, Larry will let me know. It's a very open, healthy attitude. I suppose we've learned over the years that egos have to be checked in before you walk into the studio. You can have a band ego, in fact that's essential when you're determined to make something great happen. But don't get too hung up on your own personal side of it. No one frets about whether their idea made it to the final cut or not. It's the best idea that wins out.'

Edge, in *U2 By U2* (2006).

'It's hard to have an ego when you're dealing with prisoners of conscience as an issue.'

Adam Clayton, on the 1986 Conspiracy of Hope tour, in *U2 By U2* (2006).

'To be good at something you have to be selfish and to be great at something you have to be greedy. Without that greed, you won't make it, in the sense that you want everything for your music. That's why you should never look up to pop musicians – they're all egotistical bastards, they translate their pain into song – I know that I myself am not immune to it.'

Bono, speaking on the American syndicated radio show, *RCD* (May 1992).

'I always thought that U2 would be one of a generation of great modern rock bands. In fact, we seem to be largely alone, our contemporaries have largely disappeared, or at least ceased to be rock bands in the way that I liked my rock bands to be when I was growing up.'

Paul McGuinness, *Hot Press* (11 August 1988).

'Celebrity eventually makes you look ridiculous. You could think that in such a context everyone's ego inflates dramatically. Mine ended up exploding, or rather imploding in the pathetic face of fame.'

Bono, *Libération* (9 October 2000).

'I cannot ever really comprehend what our fans see me as. I can only observe it from the eye of the storm. Probably the people who buy our records or go to our shows are far more aware of the Edge as the public person than I am. I happen to be more aware of his private side.'

Edge, *Hot Press* (30 November 1984).

'A rock star is someone with a hole in his heart almost the size of his ego.'

Bono on Bono (2005).

'I don't mean to sound arrogant but, even at this stage, I do feel that we were meant to be one of the great groups. There's a certain spark, a certain chemistry that was special about the Stones, The Who and The Beatles, and I think it's also special about U2.'

Bono, *Propaganda* (1981).

'We have a collaborative music-making process that's been established from the beginning and I couldn't possibly permit a situation where Brian Eno was making more than a member of U2. Brian is a genius but so are the band. I would think that it's a privilege and an education to work with U2 as a producer.'

Paul McGuinness, on the procedures for working on the U2 side project album, *Passengers: Original Soundtracks 1*, in *U2 By U2* (2006).

'I've never had fear of failure. Isn't that mad?'

Bono on Bono (2005).

Interviewer: 'What's the best thing about you?'

Adam: 'The way I might look at you.'

Adam Clayton, *ZooTV Tour Programme* (1992).

'I'm an outgoing sort of person, I want to take everything and break everything. I want people in London to see and hear the band. I want to replace the bands in the charts now because I think we're better.'

Bono, *Record Mirror* (November 1979).

'There is something very uncomfortable about a rich rock star being photographed with poor, starving kids. In that sense, I wish it wasn't me. I don't blame people for being cynical. I'm sure it's not all altruistic. There must be some ego involved ... I have the sort of personality where I believe I can always find a solution.'

Bono, *Q* (November 2004).

'We thought we had an ace to play whenever we needed it, which was 'Staring at the Sun'. We thought it was a solid gold number one hit. It clearly wasn't the song we thought it was

… [Island Records boss] Chris Blackwell has said the problem was there was no procedure for the record company to tell U2 to stop …'

Paul McGuinness, in *U2 By U2* (2006).

'I thought of *Zooropa* at the time as a work of genius. I really thought our pop discipline was matching our experimentation and this was our *Sergeant Pepper*. I was a little wrong about that …'

Bono, in *U2 By U2* (2006).

'He has a healthy disrespect – and respect – for his own ego.'

Bono, on Edge, in *Bono on Bono* (2005).

'I think we were a little out of touch … That was part of the problem, too. We got to Berlin and realised, "Uh, oh…" We didn't know what it was like to be in the studio and to think and it stunned everybody. We weren't as great as we figured we were.'

Bono, on the writing and recording process behind *Achtung Baby*, in Bill Flanagan, *U2 at the End of the World* (1995).

The Music Business

You start off as fresh and as green as a newly mowed lawn, and end up like a gravel path overgrown with weeds. Corruption of the innocent is putting it mildly, but it also depends on what your levels of gullibility are. If you want to make it in showbiz, it might help that you have a manager who knows (or at least seems to know) what he/she is doing. It also helps if you yourself want to bend a few personal rules for the sake of success, future or otherwise, while at the same time realising that capitalising on whatever creativity you might have accounts for nothing if you haven't got a business plan. Which, in U2's case, is known as Paul McGuinness.

'We had this idea that you should be creative in business, that you didn't have to divide it up into art and commerce. We'd meet these record company people on tour in the US and to most punk bands coming out of the UK, these were the enemy. And I didn't think they were the enemy. I thought they were workers who had gotten into music for probably all the right reasons, and weren't as lucky as we were, weren't able to fulfil their ambition to be musicians and were now working the music. Maybe they lost their love and I felt that part of our thing was to re-ignite that. So a lot of people got inspired and they rallied around us, creating a network, and that protected us, created this kind of cushion. Then you start to see organisation in a creative light. You start to say, "Well, these are important decisions, this artwork..." And you realise that, in fact, to be a group is the art.'

Bono, in Bill Flanagan, *U2 at the End of the World* (1995).

'I'm very proud of U2 and what they've achieved creatively over the years. I'm also proud of what we've achieved together in business. We always agreed that it would be pathetic to be good at the music and bad at the business.'

Paul McGuinness, in *U2 By U2* (2006).

'Paul McGuinness was an important step, and we went after him in a very determined way ... We didn't want to be a cult group, we wanted to be a big group and we thought that's where our talents lay, that's what we, as a group of guys together, had the potential to be. We needed Paul McGuinness to help us do that.'

Edge, in B.P. Fallon, *U2 Faraway So Close* (1994).

'Some of the tours went on too long. They didn't know how to stop doing what they'd had to do at the beginning, which was go at it non-stop. They had trouble learning to pace themselves. And, of course, managers tend to want bands to work. I think Paul sometimes overbooked them. Bands don't often have this kind of longevity, so one never knows how long you'll remain artistically and commercially viable. There's a tendency to say, "Okay, let's go for it, go for it, go for it." And because U2 are as ambitious artistically as they are, they want to keep trying things, and be out doing it. Testing the limits of how far it can go. There are a lot of good reasons for it, but sometimes it felt like it was time to stop, time to regenerate creatively, and time to give the public a rest, too. How can they miss you if you won't go away?'

Ellen Darst, Principle Management employee from 1983–93, in Diana Scrimgeour, *U2 Show* (2004).

'Anyone is welcome to tape our shows and pass them around to their friends. But if you start selling them, we will find out where you park your car and we will pay you a little visit!'

Bono, *Propaganda* (2000).

'I was cautious of Paul [McGuinness]. Even at our stage, there were stories of managers and record companies ripping bands off. Paul had some experience of management from his time with Spud. It seemed an odd choice for a man who was obviously bright and intelligent. But what would I know? I was still a snot-nosed kid.'

Larry Mullen Jr, in *U2 By U2* (2006).

'Paul McGuinness approached me last year and told me U2 were setting up this record label, and asked would I be interested in running it for them. And I at first was very surprised and second of all very anxious about what I would do, because I literally despise the music U2 make.'

Fachtna O'Ceallaigh, former manager of The Boomtown Rats, on being asked to run Mother Records, *Hot Press Yearbook* (1987).

'There's this kind of 'God Almighty' approach to U2 in Ireland that's really distressing. There's an aura of correctness about everything U2 does and people tend not to question or not to argue the point. And I don't think that's right, I don't think that's the way a music business should be ... I think they're definitely part of a new establishment, a U2/*Hot Press*/Radio Telefís Éireann power base that controls the direction of the music business in Ireland.'

Fachtna O'Ceallaigh, *Hot Press Yearbook* (1987).

'I regard their approach to the label as I regard their approach to everything – too precious.'

Fachtna O'Ceallaigh, *Hot Press Yearbook* (1987).

'If U2 had signed to CBS they would have died a death.'

Chas De Whalley, CBS A&R man, *Q* (June 1996).

'U2 still sell ... We're still selling more records than anyone else – and we certainly make more money touring than selling records.'

Paul McGuinness, *Hot Press* (4 October 2006).

'There were many things that set U2 apart from the rest, but maybe the most important thing was their sheer ambition. They wanted it so badly, they were ready to do as much work as it took. They were also very clear about the parameters within which they would promote themselves. There were a lot of things that they wouldn't do, like radio station IDs. "Hi, this is Bono and you're listening to WXYZ..." All the bands were out doing that, but U2 wouldn't. From the very beginning, they wanted to be in control of how they were perceived, how they were marketed; it was really personal for them. I helped fashion ways in which they could do the self-promotion, but still be true to themselves. But really, those things came from them. U2 had the instinct and I had the knowledge of the market, to be able to help them get across without cheapening them in the process.'

Ellen Darst, Principle Management employee from 1983–93, in Diana Scrimgeour, *U2 Show* (2004).

'We had a very conservative booking policy. We always wanted to sell out, so we were playing venues that were slightly too small for the band, and we wouldn't book a second day if we thought it would be only half full. That was something we did consistently through the years. We always wanted to leave every town knowing that you couldn't get into that U2 gig, it was sold out.'

Paul McGuinness, in *U2 By U2* (2006).

'[U2] are people who've refused huge sums of money for relationships with commercial companies, just because they didn't feel it was a real relationship ... A car company comes to us, offers us 23 million dollars for an old song – that's a lot of money to turn down ... We turned down another incredible sum of money from a computer firm for 'Beautiful Day'.'

Bono on Bono (2005).

'It was us against the world. We weren't gonna be part of any scene.'

Bono on Bono (2005).

'Bono always rails against what he calls the brown rice position, the hippie position on things. But he's got a lot more brown rice in him than he ever wants the world to see. He really does. Look at commercial sponsorship: I know that they've had endless philosophical discussions about it, but in the long run so far they just can't bring themselves to do it. That is ultimately a brown rice position, that's part of what we love about them.'

Bill Flanagan, MTV Networks International and author of *U2 at the End of the World*, in Diana Scrimgeour, *U2 Show* (2004).

'This band is hitting out against all the aural wallpaper we have rammed down our throats on the radio and TV every day. I am personally bloody sick of every time I switch on the radio of being blasted with this contrived crap.'

Bono, *Propaganda* (1983).

'We felt totally at odds with the mainstream culture – 'Material Girl' and the 'me' generation. We were coming in at a different angle and it's now seen as being quintessentially 1980s, but at the time it really felt like we were doing something totally different from everybody else.'

Edge, on being U2 in the 1980s, *Q* (August 2006).

'We were hit and miss. We could have three great gigs in a row and then two shite ones – the record companies would always make it to the shite gigs.'

Larry Mullen Jr, in *U2 By U2* (2006).

'I don't particularly want to work with anyone who isn't great.'

Paul McGuinness, *Irish Times Magazine* (25 August 2001).

'There's a lot of baggage carried over from the 1960s that says a musician shouldn't be a businessman because – hey, man! – you're supposed to be out there, man, just smoking the weed, putting your toes in the river, surrounded by a bunch of beautiful girls combing your hair as you watch the sun come up ... I have to say it sounds better and better now that I think about it ...'

Bono on Bono (2005).

'Any band that starts out now, U2 is the blueprint. It just is. Period. Everything that you think growing up that rock 'n' roll should be, and could be, is how these guys have done it. They've written their own rules. Drive, dedication and consistency.'

Jimmy Iovine, chairman of Interscope Records, in Diana Scrimgeour, *U2 Show* (2004).

'No other band has come anywhere as close to transcending the music business's obsessive need to turn musicians into icons.'

John Waters, *In Dublin* (25 June 1987).

'They're my clients. That's the relationship.'

Paul McGuinness, *Hot Press* (4 October 2006).

'Don't try telling them what to do unless you can demonstrate that you know something they don't. U2 inherited a world where bands were given creative control. Groups by and large have an attention span of 38 seconds, and so when they go into meetings, they tend to look at stuff and go, "Yeah, great, my head hurts now, I think I'll go and have something to drink." Which is fine. Record companies are quite happy with that kind of control. Not so with U2. No one has ever filibustered them. Ever. Guys come in and they go, "We'll soon get this passed", and twenty-four hours later they've bags under their eyes and the lads [U2] are still going, "Show us that again

there..." Whatever grisly technical detail they need to know –
and some that they don't – they'll find out how the process
works and tell you how to do it better.'

Barry Devlin, director/early producer/member of Horslips, in
Diana Scrimgeour, *U2 Show* (2004).

'Paul [McGuinness] was not a warm, fuzzy feeling ... The
most striking thing about Paul was: "I don't want to be your
friend. I'll be your manager." There was no attempt to play at
friendship. Very interesting ... My old man met Paul. Paul
speaks with the low hum of the British ascendancy, so that
means my dad immediately doesn't trust him. He was
saying, "Watch that fellah."'

Bono, in *U2 By U2* (2006).

'They knew how important it was to keep the production
paramount, keep the political message ... They haven't
allowed themselves to be sucked into that Hollywood
syndrome and become cartoons of themselves. It's an Irish
trait: you might be drinking Guinness, but you tell the truth.'

Pat Morrow, Nocturne Productions Inc., in Diana Scrimgeour,
U2 Show (2004).

'You try and brand the artist in the way that U2 are branded
– the most brilliant corporate branding I have ever seen,
without anyone ever thinking that they were being
corporately got ... You never saw a picture of U2 if it wasn't
in front of the Joshua tree. Bono was out there ... He was an
OK kind of guy because he was saying the right things ...
Brilliant piece of marketing.'

Keith Negus, *Producing Pop: Culture and Conflict in the
Popular Music Industry* (1992).

'During that [*Achtung Baby*] period, Island Records was acquired by Polygram. This was a process I was very actively involved in, because we were not only the label's biggest act, we were actually part owners of Island Records. This came about before *The Joshua Tree*, basically, because Island couldn't pay us our royalties for *The Unforgettable Fire* ... We ended up taking part of the company instead. It was a very good thing to do, as it turned out.'

Paul McGuinness, in *U2 By U2* (2006).

'The idea behind doing a cover of 'Where The Streets Have No Name' was trying to have a dig at U2's pomposity of their *Joshua Tree* era. Also, it was a fun idea to take a U2 song, a very transgressive, revered U2 song, and say, "It's showbusiness everyone, let's face facts, it's showbusiness." And then U2 started doing showbusiness anyway.'

Neil Tennant, Pet Shop Boys, *Hot Press* (August 2006).

'U2 were never dumb in business. We just had a strong sense of survival in us ... We don't sit around wondering about world peace all day long. We're not sitting around like a bunch of hippies. We're from punk rock, and we're on top of it. I wish we were more on top of it ... We are very much in charge of our own destiny, and have been always.'

Bono on Bono (2005).

'What's always impressive to me about the way they conduct their affairs is they have never lost interest in the business that surrounds them and they've never forgotten that unless their business is under control, doing the work of being U2 is not possible.'

Paul McGuinness, *Hot Press* (5 August 1983).

'That wasn't our idea, it was the record company's idea ... I don't know, I just think this is a cool thing to get away with ... and that's our job, to abuse our position to get stuff on the radio that wouldn't normally get on the radio.'

Bono, on the limited release [three weeks] of 'The Fly' single, which helped it reach number one in various charts around the world, *Vox* (April 1992).

'I don't want to be a casualty. I don't want to be bullied by the business in the future ... You can do all the best work in the world, but there's a moment where some guy can just sit there and write you in or out. I don't want to give that power to somebody.'

Bono on Bono (2005).

'We have had to deal with some bullies at a corporate level in the music business, but in the end I don't have 'Slave' written on my face, like Prince did in the early 1990s. U2 is in charge of its own destiny. We own our master tapes, we own our copyrights, we run our own show. The music business does not own us.'

Bono on Bono (2005).

'U2 a corporation? It's much more like 'Five Go Down To The Sea' and can't swim. Ruthless bastards, no. Inept sometimes, yes.'

Bono, *Hot Press* (December 1987).

'You have to admit that a rock 'n' roll band does things for its own selfish reasons – not necessarily, or not only, to supply demand and satisfy customers. We're not Lever Brothers. If U2 were to perform the number of shows the audience would like them to, you'd start to see some really bad shows, and that would be the end of the group. To supply the demand is impossible and not even that desirable.'

Paul McGuinness, Q (July 1992).

'Don't spend too much on the box and the wrapping paper. No matter how big the occasion, your loved ones just want what's inside.'

Bono, on giving the people what they really want, Q (November 2002).

'It would be pathetic to be good at the music and bad at the business. You can't expect the record company to do everything for you.'

Paul McGuinness, Irish Times Magazine (25 August 2001).

'When he [Bono] asks for my opinion about anything I always give him the truth. I figure they've enough yes-men around them, somebody should tell them the truth.'

Bob Hewson, in Bill Flanagan, U2 at the End of the World (1995).

'We constructed a new paradigm for touring, where we would sell the whole tour to a single promoter in an arrangement where we shared the profits of the tour but they would underwrite costs and put up a guarantee. We invited bids based on the assumption that it would be an outdoor-only stadium tour worldwide of about a hundred shows. What it all means in business terms is very fundamental: if you are doing a very big tour with high overheads (and we were running PopMart at a daily overhead cost in excess of $200,000) then if one show falls out, or one promoter fails to pay, it can knock the figures for the whole tour sideways. In this new arrangement, we are no longer taking that risk ourselves.'

Paul McGuinness, in *U2 By U2* (2006).

'You might as well put on a suit and tie and go work for them! There are rare exceptions when it's okay to stand beside something: Larry stood beside Harley-Davidson and put his name to that because it's an American company making something special ... But the idea of getting involved in the whole big business thing is just not interesting. It's not the right thing for a rock and roll band to do, I feel.'

Bono, speaking on the DIR Radio Network in America (8 September 1987).

'The problem is that we've never found a beer that we liked enough to be sponsored with. Guinness, we might consider.'

Edge, speaking on the DIR Radio Network in America (8 September 1987).

'Our last tour [ZooTV] cost $125,000 a day. We risked bankruptcy. This time, we thought we've got to be careful. So we've got a better deal now, a worldwide promoter, and I think we've got a way of making the numbers out of the T-shirts and all that stuff.'

Bono, talking about the PopMart tour, *Mojo* (March 1997).

'I just thank God it was Edge who lost the CD. Because if it was me, there'd have been murder over it.'

Bono, on the 'rough assembly' CD of *How To Dismantle An Atomic Bomb* that went missing under Edge's stewardship, in *U2 By U2* (2006).

Money Matters

You know the scenario by now: you form a band, get a manager and borrow money from your parents in order to get a foothold on the ladder. You make ends meet by 'borrowing' pennies from the jar of money your manager keeps in his house, and by tapping your mates for odds and ends. And then, gradually, there arrives a trickle of money which within a year or so turns into a flow. And after a few more years, the flow gains momentum and weight and becomes a flood. And before you know where you are, you've got people coming up to you wanting to be your best friend. We don't know how much dosh U2 have (and why on earth would they ever want to tell us?), but we can safely say that each of them knows where their next bottle of very expensive wine is coming from — their temperature-controlled cellars, perhaps?

'It was only after *The Joshua Tree* that we started to make money. After *The Joshua Tree*, we invested a lot of money into *Rattle And Hum*. So we saw a lot of money but never made any ... It wasn't like we did The Joshua Tree tour and then someone gave me five million dollars and said, "There you are, son, go with it." It wasn't like that at all, it was a very slow thing.'

Larry Mullen Jr, in Bill Flanagan, *U2 at the End of the World* (1995).

'It's all about imagination, nothing else is important. It's not about scale – big, small, independent, alternative, anything. Whether you earn a million dollars or lose a million dollars. None of it really matters. What matters is the work and the imagination of the work.'

Bono, *Rolling Stone* (4 March 1993).

'We had run out of cash. We finished the tour on my American Express card, and when we got home I couldn't pay the bill and they took my card away. That was a really low point. Of course, everyone in Dublin thought I was some kind of rich English person who had loads of money to subsidise U2's activities. The reality was there was no money and I didn't even have a credit card anymore.'

Paul McGuinness, reminiscing about 1982–83, in *U2 By U2* (2006).

'We have two ways of dealing with our wealth. We have what U2 does as a group – decisions that are made collectively about income – and we have our own personal responsibilities. Both we keep secret and while that doesn't absolve us from all guilt of having a lot of money in a society that doesn't have much, at least it makes us feel we're doing something worthwhile with that money. There are still contradictions to be tackled, but if I have to choose what I'm going to tackle in a day, I mustn't put it before being in a band making music. You know, it's almost harder to give away money than to earn it because of the responsibilities involved.'

Bono, *Hot Press* (December 1988).

'He was affectionately known as 'The Baron' and it was like getting blood out of a turnip trying to get paid! One always got paid, I must say that, but it could have been a week later or a month later. He was good with finance!'

Joe O'Herlihy, on Paul McGuinness, *Hot Press Yearbook* (1986).

'The money means you can do what you want. If you want to go somewhere you can go without asking anyone's permission. If you want to read a book you can buy it without asking what it costs ... We know that other people don't have that freedom and we are very lucky.'

Paul McGuinness, *Irish Times Magazine* (25 August 2001).

'There's no doubt that if you do exclusive stadium shows, you make a lot of money if they sell out. But what we did was a mixture of stadium shows and arena shows, which is the most uneconomical thing you can do.'

Edge, *Rolling Stone* (10 March 1988).

'I never bought into the cliché "I'm the artist. Keep me away from the filthy lucre and the tawdry music-business world." It's just complete horseshit! It's been going on for years ... I've grown up with a lot of these bands. Some of them are the most awful, selfish, darkest individuals you could find. And some of the people in the record company who go home to their wives at night might be people you'd rather go on vacation with. I know some incredibly inspired business people, and ethical – and I know some real assholes with a golden voice.'

Bono on Bono (2005).

'We're not going to let people rip us off. We want the money!'

Bono, when asked in 1979 how he would cope with the music business, *Q Special Edition: The 150 Greatest Rock Lists Ever* (2004).'

'All through that tour, there were little performance-art things going on around the globe for no particular reason. You could file all of this under grand madness ... costing about a grand a minute!'

Bono on the ZooTV tour, in *U2 By U2* (2006).

'There is a clear deal that we have with people who buy our records and that is: here's a shitload of money, you won't have to worry about where you're going to buy your shoes or what food is on the table ... but in return all we want is you to be fucking brave and a bit brilliant. I think that's the deal. The day we bow down to commercial pressure or sell ourselves out – by that I mean don't do the work that we actually want to do – will be a very sad day.'

Bono, *Propaganda* (1997).

'The music business markets itself by infiltrating other free media. It is very skilful at promoting its wares through radio, television and press rather than buying advertising space. I sensed there was a huge commercial opportunity with technology and information organisations, the sort whose machines we use in U2's work, to infiltrate their budgets and get our music on television in a dignified and honourable manner. So Ralph Simon [founder of Zomba Music Publishing and Jive Records, and chairman of the Mobile Music Forum] and I spent most of 2004 talking to Vodafone, Nokia, Hewlett-Packard, Intel and T-Mobile trying to find a way in which our brands could co-operate for mutual benefit without being embarrassing. I nearly pulled this off, but in the end, I couldn't sell it to the band.'

Paul McGuinness, in *U2 By U2* (2006).

'There was a proposal for the band to take sponsorship from a telephone company and make large sums of money. I was opposed to the idea. There were differing opinions in the band. There was enormous pressure to take sponsorship, because the record industry was changing and record companies were spending less and less money on marketing. It was a long hot summer for me. There was a real chance that those in favour of sponsorship would win the argument and I would be out-voted. Thankfully, it never came to that.'

Larry Mullen Jr, in *U2 By U2* (2006).

'Bono is always broke, while Larry still has his First Communion money.'

Paul McGuinness, in Bill Flanagan, *U2 at the End of the World* (1995).

'We do it now cause we can afford to do it, and to be honest whatever we can do to make touring that little bit easier, we will do ... What tends to happen is the shows start to suffer if you're wiped out by travelling forty-eight hours in a bus, when you could be actually on a plane doing the journey in three. As far as backstage, it's like we just look after people as we hope we'd be looked after at other shows. But I don't think it's ever wasteful or inappropriate for the situation.'

Edge, on justifying the expense outlay for a premier league rock band, in the RTÉ Radio One programme, *B.P. Fallon Orchestra* (1987).

'The relationship between art and commerce has always existed and I have never felt that we were the sacred artists and the people who sold our music had their hands dirtied by the filthy lucre. Artists are as greedy or as selfless as anyone else. We are in business, we are tradesmen who, in the Middle Ages, would wander from town to town selling our wares. Get over it.'

Bono, in *U2 By U2* (2006).

'I have a few nice houses now; I must admit that one of my deepest fears is that I'd become that awful person who would just buy property and leave it there, not even use it, appreciate it, when there's people sleeping in the street. That would be the sort of person I would hate as a teenager ... I know I'm a little self-indulgent now, but I will say I enjoy them ... Decadence is when you don't notice what you have around you.'

Bono on Bono (2005).

'What we sell is the experience of buying a designed, branded artefact that is not just a piece of software but also represents, in tangible form, the values of the band.'

Paul McGuinness, *The Sunday Times* (13 July 2003).

'I've loved U2 for ever, but I'm beginning to loathe them now. They're such marketing mouthpieces it's disgusting me. Paying $40 to get "early access to good seats?!"... If you're a fan-club member, you should just be able to buy two tickets through the fan club – no hassles, no Ticketmaster, no dumb passwords ... like how REAL bands do 'em – like Pearl Jam ...'

Online U2 fan, *Irish Independent* (30 January 2005).

'The circumstances surrounding what became the PopMart tour were unique for U2 in several ways, none less significant than the fact that this would be their first all-outdoor tour, playing stadiums from day one. There was also a very direct (and very rare) brief to me that this tour would be "design-led", rather than being intimidated by scale or logistics. Having proved to themselves and to the world with ZooTV that, in terms of what can be toured, "anything is possible", U2 were of a mind that the only limits to be placed on the creative ambitions of this tour were to be financial ones.'

Willie Williams, principal designer of U2 live shows since 1983, in Diana Scrimgeour, *U2 Show* (2004).

'It was a feature of McGuinness' management that we might have no money but we always seemed to find a good restaurant to eat in. He was of the Oscar Wilde school of thought: the necessities I can do without, but don't touch my luxuries.'

Edge, in *U2 By U2* (2006).

'I'd get midnight phone calls from somebody loading a plane saying, "Oh, I just discovered we need another 747 because we can't get all the steel in." I mean, we were flying pieces of steel around the world on Antonovs and 747s! You know, you can rent steel in South America, South Africa, but not us!

We were carrying our own steel in aeroplanes! It was stupid. It was the lowest point in our logistical history and I think some of our own people were way out of their depth ... For the band and for myself it was this awful feeling of waking up every morning knowing that another quarter of a million dollars had been spent. It was frightening. And we never got it under control; the tour didn't make any money.'

Paul McGuinness on PopMart, in Diana Scrimgeour, *U2 Show* (2004).

'This will sound like utter shite because people see a suite in the top of the hotel in Chicago and think it must be the most incredible place to be. But the more plush the surroundings, the poorer you feel in spirit.'

Bono, *Hot Press* (December 1988).

'I have always felt that our interests and the record company's were quite different. The record company is a source of finance for a baby band, but by attempting to have hit singles, you become a hostage to your next record. The touring base that we built up was really a means of defending ourselves from that.'

Paul McGuinness, *Propaganda* (1987).

'Don't trust anyone.'

Bono, relating the advice given to him by his father on how to handle his finances, in *Bono on Bono* (2005).

'If a U2 show is going askew, as it can, the one song you can rely on to get the room back is 'Where The Streets Have No Name'. We didn't want some sixteen-year-olds turning to each other at a U2 gig and saying "Oh, great! They're playing the song from the car ad." Now, had it been a different song from the U2 canon ... We don't want to embarrass our fans, we don't want to change the mood in which this song is perceived. In another life (as a lobbyist) I will be asking for $223 million!'

Bono, *Cara* (June 2005).

'More than most bands, we take control of the circumstances in which we perform. It's part of a process we apply to most things, of not letting luck, or indeed other people's judgements, control us. We do not hand over control to the promoters, we do not hand over control of the T-shirt business to a T-shirt company ...'

Paul McGuinness, *Propaganda* (1987).

'If 10 per cent less people had come to see us, we'd have gone bankrupt, and with those kinds of bills, you don't go bankrupt a little, you go bankrupt a lot. I can't think about it now ...'

Bono, on the PopMart tour, in *Bono on Bono* (2005).

'Phew, the roof for the house in the West of Ireland is looking good! I'll be able to change the car this year after all!'

Edge, on hearing the initial playback of 'One', in Bill Flanagan, *U2 at the End of the World* (1995).

'There was a few hundred quid in the bag. I thought: "This is amazing!" You ring a guy at the record company, ask him for money – he comes over to your hotel with a bag full of it. Welcome to the music business!'

Larry Mullen Jr, on his entry into the music industry, in *U2 By U2* (2006).

'U2's business is 90 per cent conducted around the world. 90 per cent of our tickets and 98 per cent of our records are sold outside of Ireland. It's where we live and where we work and where we employ a lot of people. But we pay taxes all over the world – of many different kinds. And like any other business, we're perfectly entitled to minimise the tax we pay.'

Paul McGuinness, answering the criticism surrounding the moving of U2's financial operations to the Netherlands, *Hot Press* (4 October 2006).

'We like to say our band is a gang of four, but a corporation of five. I understand brands, I can understand corporate America, I can understand economics. This is not at all so difficult. U2 was art school, business school. It's always the same attitude that wins the day: faith over fear. Know your subject, know your opponent. Don't have an argument you can't win.'

Bono on Bono (2005).

'They don't have to be an innovative band, in fact it probably doesn't pay them to; they'd be better off financially just settling in to a rut.'

Brian Eno, *Propaganda* (1991).

'Money is a big thing, especially if you don't have it. You have to give it respect, but you don't want to give it too much of your love. So it means we have to sit the band in rooms, when we'd rather be making music, going though boring shit. But if you do it right, it means you only have to do that once a month – or in my case once a week.'

Bono on Bono (2005).

'The biggest turn-on about having shitloads of money is the ability to do what you like. All that shite about being the biggest, the best, the loudest is meaningless. What matters is that when you're mega you can afford an independence that a lot of those so-called indie bands can't. It's a question of faith, making the leap, not believing the hype that rock 'n' roll has become.'

Bono, *The Face* (April 1992).

'Putting their money where there mouths were was always part of the way U2 did things. Sometimes with very disastrous results, with financially uncomfortable results.'

Paul McGuinness, in Diana Scrimgeour, *U2 Show* (2004).

'I don't mind paying taxes though I try to pay as little as I can, obviously – I prefer to equally distribute my own wealth ... I know how to make money, and probably have some sense in that area, but I'm not interested in it for its own sake and never have been.'

Bono, *Hot Press* (December 1988).

'We value its potential but never it.'

Edge, *Hot Press* (October 1986).

'In white music, particularly white rock in America and even indie music in England, there is a real embarrassment about talking about cash. You have these guys who are very shy, and they are like, "I don't really want to be in a band, I don't know how this happened to me; here I am, I'm successful, I'm signed to a major label, I got heavy management, but it's all a bit too much..." You don't see that in hip-hop. It's so much freer because those guys are saying, "The music is the music, but I'm also taking care of business." They are very honest about it, and they always come off like they are greedy, like it's all about money, but it's not.'

Bono, *Mojo* (March 1997).

'None of it means anything, Da, except the music. That's a gift from God and it is his to take away. If that is meant to be there is nothing we can do. And anyway, the money is invested in gilts.'

Bono, on being asked by his father what he would do if U2 ended, in Eamon Dunphy, *Unforgettable Fire – the Story of U2* (1987).

'Apple made sense. It's the coolest company around and there was no money changing hands. We all agreed it was the right company to work with and we could both benefit from this relationship. Of course, there was grumbling from what you might call the militant wing of the U2 fan base. They accused us of selling out.'

Larry Mullen Jr, on U2's iPod deal with Apple, in *U2 By U2* (2006).

Interviewer: 'If there was an extra six hours per day, what would you do with it?'

Bono: 'Charge interest.'

Bono, *ZooTV Tour Programme* (1992).

Controversy and Courts of Law

It's fair and, yes, judicious to say that U2 are not the most litigious rock band in the world. Yes, they protect their copyright and all associated with that in a way that any company or corporation would, but you never see them chase the small fry through the courts, do you? Or then again, perhaps you do. The court case involving a former stylist of the band made people wonder exactly why U2 went to so much trouble retrieving articles of clothing that were, by this stage, old and (shudder!) old fashioned. Conjecture of one sort and another is merely gossip-by-numbers — we'll probably never know the real reasons as to why Bono entered a court of law in Dublin and argued for the return of trousers, a hat and other items of attire. It remains — much like the reasons behind Larry's defiance of the laws of ageing — a mystery.

'The Department of Health announces that it will be taking legal action against U2 for their promotional concert posters in which Bono has a small cigar in his mouth – it is in breach of legislation that prohibits the use of tobacco products in advertisements.'

Pimm Jal de la Parra, *U2 Live – a Concert Documentary* (1994).

'I am disappointed that a rock star who is supposed to be a role model for young people chose to vandalise the work of another artist.'

Dianne Feinstein, Mayor of San Francisco, on Bono's spray painting the words 'Rock & Roll Stops The Traffic' on an Armand Vaillancourt statue on 11 November 1987. Bono was charged with malicious mischief, but claimed his action was borne out of artistic expression. The charges were subsequently dropped. In some Irish newspapers, Bono's father was quoted as saying that his son 'deserves anything he gets convicted of'. On 14 November, the sculptor, at the invitation of Bono, walked on stage at a U2 gig in Oakland, and sprayed the words 'Stop The Madness' on the stage.

'I am a celebrity in this country ... I don't have time to talk ... You will do yourself a lot of harm as I am well known high-up ... stop messing ... You'll be sorry for this ... I am the bass player with U2 and I want to go home to bed ...'

A selection of conversational snippets from Adam Clayton to Garda Gerard Walsh on the evening of 2 March 1984. Clayton drove through a garda checkpoint, subsequently dragging Garda Walsh along the road for over forty feet when Walsh had reached into Clayton's car to switch off the ignition. Clayton thereafter pleaded guilty to dangerous driving and driving with excess alcohol. He was disqualified from driving for two years, in Damian Corless, *Gubu Nation* (2004).

'I was an asshole. I was drunk. But it was pretty embarrassing to see it spread all over the papers.'

Adam Clayton, on the incident with Garda Walsh, *Hot Press* (October 1988).

'I bitterly regretted this incident.'

Adam Clayton, following his court case on 1 September 1989 when he faced charges of possession and intent to supply cannabis. Clayton was let off the charges; he contributed £25,000 to the Women's Aid Refuge Centre, in Damian Corless, *Gubu Nation* (2004).

'In the end it was quite a minor offence that some individuals tried to blow up into something quite serious ... When it went to court, the judge 'invited' me to donate IR£25,000 to charity in return for having no conviction on my record. I accepted his invitation. If the judge's intention was to make an example of me, I am not sure if that was the right way to do it, since the message it was sending out was just confusing. It was certainly confusing to me.'

Adam Clayton, in *U2 By U2* (2006).

'Judge Windle made it clear that he wasn't exactly an expert on rock 'n' roll ... "I don't know anything about these singing groups, but I understand that they have some influence on children, youths ... How long do they listen to this stuff – until they're about thirty, I suppose."'

Liam Fay, reporting on Adam Clayton's 1989 court case, *Hot Press* (21 September 1989).

'We tried to avoid this rather bizarre situation. It's embarrassing, it's futile. There doesn't seem to be much of a case here in our point of view. She has our stuff, it doesn't matter how she came by it. We want to prevent her from selling it because it's our stuff. It's obvious to everyone in this room that she has them and we want them back.'

Bono, on the court case between U2 and their former stylist Lola Cashman, *Irish Sun* (18 October 2006).

'How can anyone take Bono seriously? One day he is telling us how to save the world and the next he is in the Dublin High Court deep in a legal challenge – for his old hat ... Can we afford to clutter up the High Court with this type of trivia? Of course, another famous lyricist has already given us the answer: "Money, money, money, it's a rich man's world."'

Letter to *The Irish Times* (21 October 2006).

'In this day and age, the cult of celebrity has a far greater bearing on the outcome of a court case than the facts presented.'

Lola Cashman, former U2 stylist, who lost her court case against the band in relation to items of clothing (including a hat and trousers) she claimed Bono had given her, *The Irish Times* (16 November 2006).

'He may be a big star, but everything else about him is little. Bono did not go to court to get his *Rattle And Hum* hat back, he went because he was angry that I had written the book and he had never let that go. It was all about the book. I think he is terribly insecure. After the book, he was not my friend anymore and he morphed into Corporate Brand Bono ... I know they were angry about even the small details I included in the book. I believe they were concerned that I might spill more details in the future and wanted to silence me. The court case was the way to do it and they succeeded. They had the money and the power to steam-roll over a small person like me and they did.'

Lola Cashman, former U2 stylist, talking about how she thought Bono reacted to her book *Inside the Zoo with U2* (1993), *Sunday Independent* (31 December 2006).

'Let the nation rejoice: Bono's trousers have finally achieved closure.'

Miriam Lord, *The Irish Times* (16 November 2006).

'I clearly know what belongs to me and what does not.'

Lola Cashman, former U2 stylist, giving evidence in the court case between her and U2, *The Irish Times* (20 October 2006).

M: 'They even accused us of defamation of character by associating this foul language with the clean-cut image of the group U2!'

Edge: 'Ha ha ha hee hee ha.'

Edge, reacting during part of a lengthy Question and Answer session with members of Negativland, an American act who were sued by Island Records in 1991 for violation of trademark and copyright following their use of the band's name and samples from 'I Still Haven't Found (What I'm Looking For)', *Mondo 2000* magazine (summer 1992).

'Cork County Secretary Frank Murphy, acting on behalf of the GAA [Gaelic Athletic Association], bans the sale of *Achtung Baby* condoms from their merchandising stands at the concert at Cork's Pairc Ui Chaoimh venue on 24 August

1993. U2 manager Paul McGuinness responds by handing out free condoms. Later on stage, MacPhisto attempts to phone Frank Murphy, but the phone goes unanswered – Murphy is in the stadium watching the show.'

Pimm Jal de la Parra, *U2 Live – a Concert Documentary* (1994).

Dublin and Ireland

U2 formed at a time when there was no infrastructural template in Ireland for supporting a successful rock band. Previous successful Irish rock acts, such as Rory Gallagher, Van Morrison, Horslips and The Boomtown Rats, left their country for other parts of the world which could assist rather than detract from their ambitions. Yet U2 decided to stay, and to base their operations from Dublin's city centre. One could argue that Ireland's beneficial tax status for artists helped them to continue to hang around, but if you were to strongly nail home that point you might be missing out on something lodged in the band's collective mindset which is stronger than financial remuneration – loyalty, family ties, cultural belonging. And, of course, the way the models and other beautiful people might be lookin' at ya at 3 a.m. in the VIP library of Lillie's Bordello.

'U2's success and their decision to remain based in their homeland has been a decisive factor in sealing the image of modern Ireland.'

Gavin Martin, *Uncut Legends 3*.

'Beyond Ireland in the immediate aftermath of punk, artistry in rock often consisted of fracturing reality but rarely constructing its fragments. In contrast, U2 dared to transcend reality. After all, wasn't being an Irish band in the seventies, especially with their ambition, itself unreal?'

Bill Graham, *Another Time, Another Place* (1989).

'When you're away from home, in the States or wherever, all they know about you are the records or the press, so they come to you with all these false preconceptions. You're this image of Bono or Adam Clayton or whatever – and while you can try and make them relaxed, they don't really hear you. Whereas here, you can get pissed – and people have seen you pissed before. You can meet them and they don't have expectations of you being able to cure their blind granny, whereas that's kind of what happens in the States.'

Adam Clayton, *Hot Press* (October 1988).

'I've a funny feeling that it's the little things that I hate about Ireland that I secretly love. I probably like the hard times that they give us here. It makes a change. It definitely works against you rather than for you that you're in U2. People are incredibly cynical about success.'

Bono, *Propaganda* (1988).

'Their songs of innocence and of experience seem to have become enmeshed in all of our lives. They've become part of our shared memories of good times and bad. But apart from their global success, U2 have written the soundtrack for generations of Irish people.'

Gerry Ryan, 'U2 Night', a night of programmes about U2 on Ireland's RTÉ (25 June 2005).

'People in the West of Ireland couldn't care less who you are. If I was a star footballer in the Mayo team then I'd be a big celebrity but rock 'n' roll means nothing to them. These are fishermen and farmers.'

Bono, *Propaganda* (1988).

'Except for Bono, who would be hard-pressed to walk in the centre of Dublin and not get torn to shreds, the rest of us can get on with a normal life. In Ireland, I think people are proud of what we're doing, but there's no feeling of awe because they've known us for so long. They realise we're the same old assholes we always were!'

Edge, radio interview with Boston's WBCN (April 1985).

'When I was growing up, I didn't know where I came from ... I knew I was from Ballymun but I didn't know what that meant. I didn't know I was Irish until I went to America.'

Bono, in Richard Kearney (ed.), *Across the Frontiers: Ireland in the 1990s* (1988).

'You contributed to Dublin's change of image abroad but more importantly you helped change the way we saw ourselves. Dublin's current success has many fathers but I am talking today to five of them.'

Mary Freehill, Dublin's Lord Mayor, at the conferring of the Freedom of the City of Dublin to U2 and Paul McGuinness (2000).

'Father, I need a lend of £500, cos we're gonna go over to London and we're gonna score ourselves a record deal and when we get our record deal, we're not gonna stay in London, we're not gonna go to New York City. We're gonna stay and base our crew in Dublin. Cos these people, this is our tribe.'

Bono, talking from the stage at Slane Castle, Ireland (September 2001).

'There's no comparison with America or even Europe. It's a very isolated country – a totally different world. Things like abortion, contraception and pornography don't exist. You have to fight – very hard – if you want to do anything different. To be in a band is really, really difficult. There's nowhere to play. But it's an interesting and beautiful place ... I wouldn't live anywhere else. It doesn't have the pressures of rock 'n' roll. Somebody says, "There's the drummer from U2." Another person answers, "So what?" In America or anywhere else, you come out of the hotel and people want to take bits out of you. In Ireland, people have respect and they leave you alone.'

Larry Mullen Jr, *Modern Drummer* (1986).

'U2 have emerged from a place and a time – Ireland in the 1970s – which was the product of a historical and evolutionary process, and they are as faithful a representation of that place and time as it is possible to conceive of.'

John Waters, *Race of Angels – the Genesis of U2* (1994).

'We saw ourselves as Irish and saw absolutely no reason to employ American or English people to tell us how to do the rock 'n' roll business.'

Paul McGuinness, *Hot Press Yearbook* (1986).

'I just love the retreat of Dublin and Ireland. It has given me the best of both worlds, to go out and play at being a star, even though I don't think I particularly look like one or act like one off the stage. But then, when I want my other life back, I get it in Dublin ...'

Bono on Bono (2005).

'I don't see as much of [Dublin] as I used to. When I was seventeen ... I used to go down and pretend I was a student at Trinity and get the subsidised lunches ... I really got into Dublin then. Now, I don't feel as free just to roam the city. If I do it now it's usually after 2 a.m.'

Bono, *Propaganda* (1988).

'U2 grew up in a context that was not merely external to the cultural entity that was Ireland, but external to the Dublin of the time as well. You might say that they developed as a reaction to both.'

John Waters, *Race of Angels – the Genesis of U2* (1994).

'So far all the press has been great, the best of our career. You could get the impression that everybody loves what we're doing. But you watch what happens next. Watch what happens when we get to England. And wait for Dublin. Come home with us and get another perspective. Come home for our beheading.'

Bono, on media responses to the ZooTV tour, in Bill Flanagan, *U2 at the End of the World* (1995).

'I've travelled around the world as Clannad's manager playing gigs in different places, and people would say to me, "Where are you from?" and I'd go, "I'm from Ireland." They'd say, "Oh, you're the fucking IRA. Aren't you guys over there killing one another?" I remember the significant change which came, that in telling someone where I was from they now said, "Oh, that's where U2's from." I thought, "Jesus, they've passed the fucking IRA in terms of world recognition." The country suddenly went from being known as a battleground to being the home of U2. That's how important they became, and we got a chance to go out there, be Irish and not just be associated with war. They changed the perception of [Ireland] internationally in such a positive way.'

Dave Kavanagh, U2's first agent, in Diana Scrimgeour, *U2 Show* (2004).

'It is part of our national inferiority complex to believe that we can only be invaded, we cannot invade. Therefore, a band as popular, creative and successful as U2 could only have originated here by accident.'

John Waters, *The Irish Times* (4 March 1997).

'Everyone from the [Boomtown] Rats has left the country really bitter. I won't leave this country bitter at all. The plan is that if we have to leave – and we're still not sure – it will be only for a while. It's basically that we feel the group has to be thrown into different circumstances if it's going to be stimulated, if it's going to change. It would be very easy to stay here. But we'll go – and we have to come back.'

Bono, *NME* (22 March 1980).

'Alternately stark and spectacular, their music, lyrics and imagery reflect the alienation and striving of a generation ... For Irish-American kids, still struggling for their place in American society, U2 have been a beacon.'

Dubliner (June 2005).

'The Irish can really relate to the black people. They say the Irish are the white blacks – I mean, we like to think we have the same soul. We definitely share the same sort of spirit of 'up against all odds we'll do it'.'

Bono, *Propaganda* (1987).

'U2 are Paddys with attitude.'

John Waters, *Race of Angels – the Genesis of U2* (1994).

'Dublin's in a constant state of amber.'

Bono, *Record Mirror* (November 1979).

'Irish people are not cool – they're hot ... Passionate, Latin. We're like Latin people who can't dance or dress!'

Bono, *Sydney Sun-Herald* (November 2006).

Beginnings

The past, we have been informed on a regular basis, is a different country. But if you're a reasonably smart sort of person, you'll realise that what you are at this moment of your life is because of how you were formed from a very early age. We'd wager that U2 are the kind of people intelligent enough to realise that to lose sight of where you came from is to lose sight of what you are. Family, in particular, is crucial to their sense of balance, be it Bono's memories of ongoing arguments with his father (now deceased), Larry's sense of maternal loss, Adam's struggle to achieve long-lasting love or Edge's recent battle in coping with a family illness.

'I remember on one occasion we had an awful row. I gave him a few thumps and threw him out in the hall and closed the door. I opened the door and I heard this sniggering. I looked and there was a banana skin and he was sitting on the stairs waiting for me ... Ah, he was exasperating, he really was. But there was nothing bad in him. He was living in his own world and we were sort of superfluous to it. And it still applies today. He was an extraordinary kid. He was very hard to nail down. We couldn't get him to study when he was in school, just could not get him to study. He'd go off to study and the next thing you'd hear him strummin' the guitar.'

Bob Hewson on Bono, in Bill Flanagan, *U2 at the End of the World* (1995).

'It was very James Joycean. Or like the Wu-Tang Clan.'

Edge, on his and Bono's nicknames, *Vanity Fair* (November 2004).

'The early years were all about making ends meet. The manual for starting a young band is pretty much the same the world over: you begin in your dad's garage, you climb the ladder to the school hall, you depend upon your parents to bring your band gear around in their cars, you work as hard as you can and you just hope for the chance of that big break. That is exactly what it was like, even for U2, at the beginning.'

Joe O'Herlihy, U2's audio director since 1979, in Diana Scrimgeour, *U2 Show* (2004).

'He used to wear a long sheepskin Afghan coat, he had tinted glasses and he smoked. Some people were saying to me, "You know that weirdo in the Afghan coat? He has a bass." It didn't matter if he could play it. Adam was in.'

Larry Mullen Jr, in *U2 By U2* (2006).

'I wanted to manage them because I thought they could be a very big group. There are bands who legitimately wish to do nothing more than play at weekends, and there are other bands who implicitly want to do what great bands have done, and I suppose U2 were always in that category. They always wanted to be a great band, and it was clear from the beginning that anything short of that was going to be a disappointment. We were sanguine enough I suppose in the beginning to know that the odds against that were very high but we were all nonetheless prepared to try.'

Paul McGuinness, *Hot Press Yearbook* (1986).

'The tape, recorded in March, was a dazzling account of a band with quite amazing potential. Demos have an annoying habit of falling into narrow, obvious categories these days; for the most part they're fad-conscious or just plain incompetent. The U2 tape, however, was different. Here was a band that defied trends, blends or bombast, a band that revealed direction, assurety and downright arrogance, letting you know from the Mickey Mouse confines of a C-60 cassette that they had something vital to contribute to the rock and roll of 1979.'

Dave McCullough, on potential and possibilities, *Sounds* (15 September 1979).

'We were four completely different people, four people going nowhere and we decided to go there together. Four rejects, on all different levels, from the system. Four people – four intelligent people – who probably wouldn't be accepted for the ESB or the civil service. The only thing we had in common was the music, but there was, and is, quite an odd unity.'

Bono, *Hot Press* (18 August 1983).

'To be perfectly honest, I thought they were fucking, raving lunatics! The musical content was nil. They had to play their own music because they couldn't play anyone else's!'

Joe O'Herlihy, U2's audio director since 1979, on his first impressions of U2, Hot Press Yearbook (1986).

'I was the boy who wouldn't turn the other cheek. But I never liked the violence. Never. I would worry myself sick about having to go out on the street, in case another teenager I had been in a mill with would come back for more.'

Bono, in U2 By U2 (2006).

'I'll pay you back, Dad, if it takes me one year or ten.'

Larry Mullen Jr, talking to his father on the latter's contribution of £100 towards a make-or-break visit to London in October 1979, in Eamon Dunphy, Unforgettable Fire – the Story of U2 (1987).

'Dave Edge is a superlative guitarist and he'll improve so much, being so young, being so bright, so good. U2 have created a unique and identifiable sound of their own. It's a good sound, one that's adding nuances to pop and metal, without being either one exclusively.'

Review of one of U2's famed Dandelion Car Park gigs, Hot Press (August 1979).

'When Paul came to me in 1978 and said, "I'm thinking of managing another band." I said, "You're crazy. I beseech you don't do this ..." He said, "Well, I don't agree with you. I think these guys are very good." Paul asked me if I'd go into the studio with them, so I agreed. After I came out of the studio I told him: "Two things: (1) you have to get a proper producer; and (2) you have to mortgage the house." I'd been in a band. I knew what made bands tick. What defines great bands is the kind of glue between members. There has to be a degree of compatibility, a degree of imagination, but most of all there's their own sense of where they can go together as a unit. That was the single thing that I saw uniquely in them, and I was right ... These guys had 'Great Group' written all over them. They were striped like zebras.'

Barry Devlin, director/early producer/member of Horslips, in Diana Scrimgeour, *U2 Show* (2004).

'1978 was the first I'd probably heard of U2 and I got involved because I played their demo tapes, and they were one of those bands that I was trying to help along ... Looking back it's very easy to say, "Oh, we all knew Bono had it." No, we didn't. But we certainly knew he was a bit more of a chancer, which is what was needed.'

Dave Fanning, Dublin-based radio/television presenter, in Diana Scrimgeour, *U2 Show* (2004).

'Clayton, you are an ass ... a complete washout.'

The headmaster at Dalkey's Castle Park boarding school, 1975–76, to Adam Clayton, in Eamon Dunphy, *Unforgettable Fire – the Story of U2* (1987).

'It was the Larry Mullen Band for about ten minutes, so as not to hurt my feelings ... Then Bono came in and that was the end of that. He blew any chance I had of being in charge.'

Larry Mullen Jr, in *U2 By U2* (2006).

'They seemed to ask the right questions. The Boomtown Rats had dominated Dublin's post-punk scene. Bands still tried to be punks – the Radiators From Space excepted – with this negative, provincial attitude. But not U2. They also knew that Irish acts basically don't work by copying UK artists; by the time you've signed a deal, the movement has moved on. So you have to create a space of your own, and they had the capacity to do that. Even then, they were always good at making the next step. Other bands couldn't make the first.'

Bill Graham, Irish music journalist, on the band's early days, Q (June 1996).

'The Artane Boys' Band was too rigid for me. I was in for three days, and they told me to get my hair cut. And at the time, it was my pride and joy – you know, shoulder length golden locks. So I got it cut a few inches and they told me to cut it more. So I told them to stick it and I left.'

Larry Mullen Jr, Modern Drummer (1986).

'If I didn't have an outlet for my own madness I would probably just take it home with me and end up driving them all out. Sometimes at home ... I feel a little like a tourist ... they get on so well without me.'

Bono, in B.P. Fallon, U2 Faraway So Close (1994).

'My mother must have suspected I had an ear for music because she bought me a little Spanish guitar when I was seven years old. For me, this was completely fascinating. I couldn't tune it, I didn't even know how to hold it, but it was so cool – that much I did know.'

Edge, in U2 By U2 (2006).

'When we started off as a group, the last thing we wanted was to sound like anyone else. In fact, we rejected rock and roll in the old sense ... we really rejected it because so many bands back there on Baggot Street in the strip in Dublin were playing this music into the ground. With U2 we wanted to develop an original sound and bring a new point of view to rock and roll, and I think we've done that.'

Bono, in a radio interview with WBCN (April 1987).

'When they started, I didn't really want to go and see them play. I didn't like the idea of punk rock. They were brilliant, but very coarse. In a way, they were doing exactly what they do now. Only badly.'

Paul McGuinness, *Vanity Fair* (November 2004).

'The time that I knew I was capable of all the things that I disliked the most in other people was, oddly enough, one of the most joyful moments: when our first child was born. And I just felt this love for this beautiful little girl who was so fragile and so vulnerable. Some point that week, I started to understand why wars are fought. I started to understand why people were capable of cruelty in order to protect themselves and their own. And I was very humbled to realise that.'

Bono on Bono (2005).

'I distinctly remember thinking that this guy was either going to be Bowie, a massive rock icon, or Alex Harvey, and burn out after a couple of albums.'

Chas De Whalley, CBS A&R man, on an early sighting of Bono, *Q* (June 1996).

'He had some excitement going, even then, because in the middle of rehearsals there was screaming outside and girls trying to climb over the garden wall. And I remember him doing a novel thing – he took the hose to them! Which he has been doing ever since.'

Bono, on Larry Mullen Jr, in *U2 By U2* (2006).

'U2 tours were always family affairs. There was always room for the families ... Tours were booked around school holidays, and it was very much taken into account.'

Paul McGuinness, *Hot Press* (4 October 2006).

'I don't think being a pop star is any more cocooned than living in a semi-detached house with suburban lawns. I think that's just as detached from the real world. They're as bad and as good as each other. I came from that background.'

Bono, *Propaganda* (1987).

'I saved up my cash from mowing lawns to buy my first drumkit; Edge attempted to build guitars and Adam already had a bass. But Bono was slightly in dire straits and we wanted him to play guitar, although he insisted on singing. Now we know why – because he didn't have to buy or move any equipment.'

Larry Mullen Jr, *Rhythm Magazine* (1993).

'My daughter Sian. She is incredible. She's just coming out of her abstract expressionist phase.'

Edge, on being asked who his favourite artist is of the past twenty years, *Q* (November 2006).

'There was the Edge ... Edge would only take his guitar out on formal occasions – not a man to sleep with it ... And then

there was Adam, who was the guy who would wear a dress
into school or take his clothes off when we were rehearsing.
He was always into vibing people out. Into blowing heads.
And there was Larry. It's Larry's fault – he did start it ... I'm
the singer in the group U2 and people expect things from me
that I can't quite honestly give them – which is to be the life
and soul of the party. There are nights when I'll stand up on
the table and I'll take my clothes off and there'll be another
night when I'm afraid to even sit down.'

Bono, *Hot Press* (18 August 1983).

'I remember I brought him over to the US to see us play, and
I told one of the spotlight operators to get ready. I introduced
this guy – "it's his first time in America, here's my father, he's
come to see us play" – and 20,000 people turned around,
and he just stands up and gives me the finger.'

Bono, *Rolling Stone* (March 2003).

'A good investment, wasn't it?'

Mr and Mrs Evans on buying a young Edge a toy guitar, *Q*
(January 1993).

'It was the least bad of the bunch. We thought about it for a
few days and said, "Well, it's better than The Hype, why don't
we just go for it for the moment."'

Edge, on the choosing of the band name, in *U2 By U2*
(2006).

'My dad trusted no one. You know, every person knocking on
the hall door after midnight is an assassin, every girl is a
groupie. Every friend is a weirdo. Every record-business

person is a hustler and a thief. Now, how could he have known all of this?'

Bono, in *U2 By U2* (2006).

'U2 aren't interested in gang-bangs, New York pimps, whips and furs, high-fashion queens or indeed the British counter revolution. Bono's testimony is that after acne comes anguish, songs about backseat lovemaking at sixteen which is substituted at eighteen by wider spiritual insecurities ... U2 are unmarked by sin, exuberant because they retain innocence.'

Bill Graham, *Hot Press* (March 1979).

'I started [drumming] at about nine; I used to play piano. The teacher was a really nice lady, but one day she said, "Larry, you're not going to make it." She suggested I try something else.'

Larry Mullen Jr, *Modern Drummer* (1986).

'It was one of the most amazing buzzes, a huge shot of adrenalin. In that ten minutes, a world opened up of how things could be. I had a great sense of power, being in front of an audience and seeing that there was a relationship, there was something that went off, an energy. I thought a riot had taken place – and maybe it had.'

Adam Clayton, on the first gig in their school's gym, in *U2 By U2* (2006).

'Violence is the thing I remember most from my teenage years and earlier. This was a working-class area that we lived in ... but you know, the difference between the incomes of people who lived here and who lived there might be very little. It might be, like, a car. My old man had a car, so we were rich. And that was a reason to be tortured.'

Bono on Bono (2005).

'I had a feeling of the house being pulled down on me. My mother died and then there were just three men living on their own in a house. That is all it was then, it ceased being a home. It was just a house with three men killing each other slowly, not knowing what to do with our sense of loss and just taking it out on each other.'

Bono, in *U2 By U2* (2006).

'I come from a long line of salespeople on my mother's side, so I have no problem ringing the doorbell and asking people to let me in. Until I show them the Tupperware, that is.'

Bono, *The Independent* (16 May 2006).

'We came from nowhere. We came from this place that was just grey concrete. Lower middle class, a ghetto of non-culture.'

Bono, *From a Whisper to a Scream* television series (2000).

'We were wildly inconsistent. Certain shows were fantastic and others were Godawful, and we were capable of both on any given night and never really knew which way it could go.'

Edge, *Mojo* (July 2005).

'Before the show, we decided to go and get drunk, because we knew that was what you did when you were in a rock band. So, as appalling as we normally were, we were just indescribably bad, and the sound was atrocious. We were in this tiny little prefab scout hut and we couldn't afford a proper PA. We recorded the show and a couple of days afterwards we listened to it in utter disbelief ... Bono was just bellowing and all you could hear was this really distorted noise that sounded like the early Stooges. Unfortunately, I think we were playing an Eagles song.'

Edge, describing an early U2 show, in *U2 By U2* (2006).

'When my father died I went on a short vacation, which turned into a euphemism for 'drinks outing'. I don't like to abuse alcohol – anything you abuse will abuse you back – but it's fair to say I went to Bali for a drink.'

Bono on Bono (2005).

'It was my father who suggested I put a notice up on the school board for fellow musicians. We didn't always see eye to eye but through it all he was watching my back, he was figuring, "Okay, the kid wants to play drums, how do I help him survive and navigate this because he's never going to be a brain surgeon."'

Larry Mullen Jr, in *U2 By U2* (2006).

'[Friends] are family. If you're smart you create a world where you shrink in size and then you find oxygen and room to manoeuvre. If you're not, then you shrink your world and tower above it, which is my experience of a lot of folk. I think I just said I was smart there – sorry about that.'

Bono, *Q* (July 2001).

'The first link in the chain was a visit to the local jumble sale where I purchased a guitar for a pound. That was my first instrument ... The next stage was a note on the school board to the effect that "Larry had wasted a lot of money on drums and was interested in finding other people to waste money on guitars" and stuff like that, so we all met in his kitchen one day. It was Larry's kitchen so he was sort of in charge, but he was only really interested in playing drums.'

Edge, *Propaganda* (1982).

'At first, we were all going nowhere, and decided to go there together. Then something very special started to develop between us. It was a kind of brotherhood, with a loyalty to each other and a belief that we could go all the way. Before we could play, before we could write songs, before we could perform, we believed in ourselves as a band.'

Edge, in *U2 By U2* (2006)

What U2 Say About U2

Just because they love each other doesn't mean to say they don't talk dirty about each other. If anyone has an opinion of the members of U2, then it's the members of U2. They know each other fairly well by this stage, after all. Like all groups of old friends, they snipe at each other, they're smart-arse with each other, they goad each other and they protect each other. What can anyone say about what U2 say about U2, other than they're a nice bunch of guys who occasionally get on each other's nerves? With gloves off.

'I'm actually in awe of Larry for knowing exactly who he is. I don't know if I'm this or that or what. But why can't I be all of them?'

Bono, in Bill Flanagan, *U2 at the End of the World* (1995).

'Edge is the unsung hero ... I have learnt never to under-estimate him. He is dogged and relentless in the search for the perfect song, the perfect sound, the perfect idea, always looking for inspiration. Not many people know what's underneath that cool exterior.'

Larry Mullen Jr, in *U2 By U2* (2006).

'We built this band around a spark – we could only play three chords when we started, but we knew there was an excitement within the four people, and even when playing to just ten people we seemed to communicate that. We put our lives on the line and just kind of went for it.'

Bono, *Melody Maker* (6 February 1982).

'He takes far too much on, I think, but it is hard to criticise him because his political achievements are very real. But there are times when it makes the rest of the band feel that they're taking second place. I suspect they think U2 should be more important to him than it sometimes is.'

Paul McGuinness, on Bono, in *U2 By U2* (2006).

'He thrives under pressure. I'd rather he disappeared for a few days and came back inspired than hang around the studio like a caged lion.'

Edge, on Bono, *Mojo* (December 2000).

'One thing about U2 – too much is never enough.'

Larry Mullen Jr, in *U2 By U2* (2006).

'The others don't count me as a musician. In fact, the only way to get Edge to play the guitar is when I start playing it. Edge thinks that the guitar is a bit of a stupid instrument. Well, it's not the instrument that he thinks is stupid, he thinks most guitar players are, because they all sound the same or like someone else. He is almost embarrassed about being a guitar player because when I pick up the guitar and start to play, then he goes, "Maybe I'll just play it ..."'

Bono, *Mojo* (March 1997).

'Bono is chairman and founding member of Over-Achievers Anonymous. He has an irrepressible drive to be great and a lust for life. He wants to experience it all, which actually makes him very vulnerable. I sometimes worry that the media has created a myth about who he is and what he stands for. I hope the hype doesn't stop people realising that he is just a man who is trying to find himself.'

Edge, in *U2 By U2* (2006).

'It's just about self-respect. Not wanting to be flying around in an Airbus packing a lame album. Be brilliant or fuck off. We're all very fortunate, blessed, filthy rich, whatever you wanna call it, so we don't have to do it. So if we're going to do it, it better be for the purest reasons.'

Bono, *Mojo* (July 2005).

'U2's not a particularly great name.'

Larry Mullen Jr, *Q* (November 2002).

'There's a sense of unity that I don't see in many other groups. I think we take responsibility for each other in a way that most groups don't. We, as a group collectively, probably are not incredibly talented musically, but what we do is cover for one another ... No one is left with egg on their faces because there's three other guys in the band who are willing to make sure that that's not gonna happen.'

Edge, radio interview with WBCN (April 1985).

'There is a real lack of understanding about what we are, the band members and myself. We're all either seen as saint or sinner, when we're all of us – not just the band – a mixture of both. A lot of people seem to me to write about caricatures of U2. Nobody shades in the fact that I'm curious ... I think it's quite amazing that people don't understand that.'

Bono, *Hot Press* (December 1988).

'Thirty years on, I trust Bono. That's his job. I think on a night by night, gig by gig basis, he's a pretty good judge of this stuff.'

Adam Clayton, in *U2 By U2* (2006).

'We're very lucky. Bono is a natural front man. I'm a guy who wants to deal with a problem and wrestle it to the ground. Larry is one of those nuts-and-bolts kind of guys who wants to tell it like it is; he's not going to take a step unless he knows where he's going, so he's a great anchor. And Adam is our great jazzman. Whenever things are getting too square, he'll throw a curveball at us and send us in a different place.'

Edge, *Vanity Fair* (November 2004).

'We're probably not good enough to repeat our best moments, although we try occasionally. I think we make better music and have better ideas now. No Greatest Hits tour just yet.'

Larry Mullen Jr, in *U2 By U2* (2006).

'Larry is not moved by anything intellectual, he's moved by something much higher, which is instinct. But it can be so annoying.'

Bono, in *U2 By U2* (2006).

'The perception is that if you say "hold on a minute" it means "no". It's not about that. I suppose I think differently from the other three guys in the band. I don't like to make decisions quickly. In the excitement of a moment, people agree to do things that are not good for the band and not good for them, and I try to protect the band as much as I can.'

Larry Mullen Jr, on being cast as the band spoilsport, *Q* (July 2001).

'The Edge – let's just say he's on the border between something and nothing.'

Bono, on Dave Evans' nickname, *Propaganda* (1983).

'If you can't be fanciful about your art, then you're really betraying the people who have given you your freedom in the first place. Be true to who you are and what you do and run with it, and run amok with it, and I think we've always done that. As annoying as it can be. At least we're not dull.'

Bono, *Hot Press Yearbook* (2002).

'I remember Adam's room ... It was like a nightclub, by age sixteen. He had ultraviolet light ... incense burning, albums everywhere, and a soft chair. Oh yeah, I'd never seen a room like Adam's.'

Bono on Bono (2005).

'There are probably people who play guitar better but there's nobody who does it as well as me because I am me. There's nobody as good at being Keith Richards as Keith Richards. There's nobody as good at being U2 as U2 ... I don't think I'm a particularly talented guitar virtuoso. My talent, if it's anything, is my approach to the guitar by the use of effects, by non-acceptance of the usual approaches to the guitar.'

Edge, *Hot Press* (30 November 1984).

'His faith is his anchor and I think that's what enables him to navigate his way through and come out relatively unscathed. The more successful and famous he becomes outside U2, the harder it is to get an opportunity to talk and hang out the way we used to, but that's life.'

Larry Mullen Jr, on Bono, in *U2 By U2* (2006).

'U2 is an original species, we're not part of the new karaoke, there are colours and feelings and emotional terrain that we occupy that is ours and ours alone, and we're constantly trying to expand it. I think I'm finally realising how great it is to be in a group and to not fuck it up by trying to do everything else.'

Bono, *Q* (February 1998).

'Larry is always there to steady the ship when it is heading for the rocks and I have my telescope pointing the other direction, Bono is hanging off the rigging and Adam is pottering about in the engine room.'

Edge, in *U2 By U2* (2006).

'Larry is the squeaky wheel in U2 that always has to be serviced and oiled before you can roll along. He is the voice of doom, always questioning the wisdom of what we are planning. He is not always right, but he's right often enough to make him worth the effort.'

Paul McGuinness, in *U2 By U2* (2006).

'He had been expelled from an upper-class public school in Ireland, and arrived at this free school with a posh accent, wearing a kaftan that he had picked up on his holidays at age sixteen, hitching through Afghanistan ... His hair was corkscrew blond, but in an Afro. He looked like a negative of Michael Jackson.'

Bono, on Adam Clayton, in *Bono on Bono* (2005).

'He is very good at figuring out what he wants and how to get it. He has absolute dedication to achieving his goals. There are certain things you think it might be prudent for him not to do, but he's a grown-up. He knows his business.'

Adam Clayton, on Bono, *Q* (November 2004).

'There's nothing set in stone. I mean, we are the most unfocused, disorganised band as far as getting it together in the studio. We are so untogether. But that's the beauty of it. There's no formula. We don't know how to do this. People often ask, "Why don't you do some stuff like you did on *The Joshua Tree.*" The truth is, we couldn't. We wouldn't know how to repeat ourselves. We're actually not good enough to do it.'

Larry Mullen Jr, on U2's creative personality, *PopMart Tour Programme* (1997).

'The thing that the three of them have − in excessive amounts − is integrity. They are capable of, on a regular basis, walking away from huge sums of money for doing the simplest things ... They're unbendable in that sense − flexible, but not bendable.'

Bono, on U2, in *Bono on Bono* (2005).

'Whatever you do, don't get in a car with Bono – he's not great at the old driving. It's not a good look for him.'

Larry Mullen Jr, *Q* (November 2000).

'In those days we hunted as a pair. Paul [McGuinness] and I would do the record company things, we'd do the journalist things, we'd be visible, we'd have a profile, and we'd know what was going on. After The Unforgettable Fire tour I realised that my position was actually becoming destructive to the band position. I felt Paul's wishes for what the band should do were not necessarily the best decisions artistically and that the band needed my support artistically, and by then spiritually as well. Certainly, I needed to listen to that voice more, and I felt at that stage I had more in common with the three guys ... So that did change and that was tough on all of us. It was certainly tough on me and Paul to separate that way. But we'd started to move in different worlds. His world was much more grown-up schmoozing, much more dinner parties and lunches. I couldn't do those things and contribute to the band, cause so much of those things are about telling stories against the band, really. They're about stories people in bands shouldn't say about each other ... I had to protect the mystery of the band, and I couldn't do that as Paul's sidekick.'

Adam Clayton, in Bill Flanagan, *U2 at the End of the World* (1995).

'Bono was a great personality but I also knew he was a chancer, so on one level I was impressed but on another I knew he didn't always have the ability to back it up.'

Edge, on Bono in the band's early days, in *U2 By U2* (2006).

'I'm a scribbling, cigar-smoking, wine-drinking, Bible-reading band man. A show-off ... who loves to paint pictures of what I can't see. A husband, father, friend of the poor and sometimes the rich. An activist travelling salesman of ideas. Chess player, part-time rock star, opera singer, in the loudest folk group in the world.'

Bono on Bono (2005).

'He's pragmatic and no-frills and sometimes he overdoes that ...'

Paul McGuinness, on Larry Mullen Jr, *Irish Times Magazine* (25 August 2001).

'I don't care about gigs – I care about, y'know, us. If there's a choice, I'm not going to put the people, however much they're paying, before me mates.'

Bono, *Q* (March 1997).

'U2 is a four-legged table. If one of the legs gets dented, the whole thing doesn't fall down; the other three can support it.'

Larry Mullen Jr, *Vanity Fair* (November 2004).

'Adam always loved nudity. He's always been that way. He, when we were in school, used to streak down the corridor, naked.'

Bono on Bono (2005).

'You can't be incognito with Bono.'

Adam Clayton, *Propaganda* (1989).

'He was the star. When he sat behind the kit, definitely, the room changed temperature. There was something going on.

He played the drums like his life depended on it. And I think, in some very real way, that was true.'

Bono, on Larry Mullen Jr, in *Bono on Bono* (2005).

'I get the impression he's not functioning on all cylinders. He doesn't have anything important to say, anyway.'

Larry Mullen Jr, on Adam Clayton, *Q* (January 1993).

'He arrived with a bass guitar and a bass amp, and he looked incredible. He had all the gear, had all the right terminology. He looked funky, he acted funky. We didn't realise at the time that he couldn't play a note. And so big was his bluff that we looked pretty much everywhere else to why we were sounding so shit. Him!'

Bono, on Adam Clayton, in *Bono on Bono* (2005).

'I read a lot of rubbish about U2. Sometimes, when I see us described in some mythic sense or called corporate masters of our own destiny, I have to laugh out loud. Being in U2 is more like riding a runaway train, hanging on to it for dear life.'

Larry Mullen Jr, in *U2 By U2* (2006).

'The reason why agonised over everything, over every commitment, including a commitment to the band, was because he takes these contracts – verbal, emotional or otherwise – very seriously in life. He is not a messer ... It's an amazing strength to be in a room with somebody who couldn't tell a lie. It gives them a lot of power. So to maintain this position, he moves very slowly in any direction but rarely has to retreat; when he wins ground he keeps it.'

Bono, on Larry Mullen Jr, in *U2 By U2* (2006).

'He's by far the most cautious person in the band, and does not want to set out on the journey until he has a clear idea of where we're going and how we might get there. How old-fashioned! You know, he's the most sensible man in the band in that sense.'

Bono, on Larry Mullen Jr, in *Bono on Bono* (2005).

'Sometimes, I think being in U2 is being in one long meeting. Your own life is just a tea break between meetings.'

Adam Clayton, *Vanity Fair* (November 2004).

'People say, "Why don't you do interviews? What do you think about this? What do you think about that?" My job in the band is to play drums, to get up on stage and hold the band together. That's what I do. At the end of the day that's all that's important. Everything else is irrelevant.'

Larry Mullen Jr, in Bill Flanagan, *U2 at the End of the World* (1995).

'Edge only wakes up after midnight – he's an owl.'

Bono, *Q* (July 2001).

'He is a life force – he has put an awful lot more into this world than he is ever going to get out. He is a giver.'

Paul McGuinness, on Bono, *Irish Times Magazine* (25 August 2001).

'Everyone knows he is a renaissance man; throughout his life, he has seized every opportunity that came his way, be it in the band or outside the band. Sometimes, that can be very difficult to work with.'

Paul McGuinness, on Bono, *Irish Times Magazine* (25 August 2001).

'Edge is a wiser man than I am, more meditative. I have total admiration for the way he's able to keep his feelings, ego, et cetera, under control, and yet that's my biggest worry for him.'

Bono on Bono (2005).

'Bono loves nothing better than being in the spotlight and I don't think anyone else [in the band] is that interested in it.'

Edge, *Q* (July 2001).

'Edge is much more the spirit in the room the later it gets. There's a phrase after midnight that puts the fear of God into producers and engineers. It's when he says: "I have a little idea I'd like to try." That might mean they're up through to 6 a.m.'

Bono on Bono (2005).

'Some people would say I'm lucky. I'd say ... I'm lucky!'

Larry Mullen Jr, on his body's apparent lack of ageing, *Q* (July 2001).

'We fight and argue all the time! But I have to say that through it all Bono has always been there. And that was where it started, that was the original connection. When I was in deep shit, he was there, he made himself available for me, he was around. Even on the road when I was going through a rough time, I used to share a room with him. He used to make sure I was okay. It was a bit like babysitting ...'

Larry Mullen Jr, in Bill Flanagan, *U2 at the End of the World* (1995).

'If you're just another arsehole from the suburbs, I think it's pretty understandable if one was offered a chance to take on the world and win, you'd go for it. I wasn't destined for greatness in any other area. I'd have ended up being some kind of bad landscape gardener or something. I much prefer this.'

Adam Clayton, *Q* (July 2001).

'It's like being in a street gang. And it's all very well being in a street gang when you're sixteen, but it's bloody weird when you're thirty-two.'

Edge, *Q* (September 1993).

'There are four members of U2. If there is a fifth, non-musical, member it is Paul McGuinness. Either that or Adam's willie!'

Bono, in B.P. Fallon, *U2 Faraway So Close* (1994).

'I'm the most untogether person I know. In the band, they just say, "Here comes chaos." I want to be together – it's my ambition to one day get my own life in order and tie it up with string and be as organised as somebody like Adam Clayton ... Clayton's unbelievable. Field Marshall Clayton! For a guy who can stay out all night, if he needs to be up at eight o'clock, he'll be there at eight o'clock on the button.'

Bono, radio interview with WBCN (April 1987).

'Adam has an incredible soul, the unlikely conscience of the band. During the early days, when the rest of us were at the height of our Christian fervour, Adam was actually the most Christian in his tolerance and humanity. In some ways, because he is the one who doesn't have to worry so much about the music or the lyrics, he has a freedom to contribute things you would never have thought of, to throw in something that is way outside of the discussion. He is our wild card, naturally avant-garde.'

Edge, in *U2 By U2* (2006).

'It's one day at a time – it's never that spontaneous – but it is one year at a time.'

Bono, *Q* (January 1993).

'I am Bono and I'm sick of him. I really am. But there are a lot of Bonos. Some annoy me more than others. Like Van Morrison said, "I'll be great when I'm finished."'

Bono, *Q* (November 2004).

'Each other and self-criticism, mutually relentless self-criticism.'

Paul McGuinness, on being asked what has kept U2 together for so long, *Vanity Fair* (November 2004).

'It's great if people get comfort from what we do. Great. What more could you ask for from a pair of shoes? But that's what we do. It's not what we are ... The Bono I know is a lot crazier than the Bono people see on stage ... We all have our own demons and his ones are bigger than everyone else's.'

Adam Clayton, *Hot Press* (October 1988).

'Some people have described us as a band that soars above reality and we're hanging in the air somewhere. I think this band refuses to admit the existence of ordinariness.'

Edge, in a syndicated US radio interview (December 1984).

'This thing doesn't have to go on forever. And it might not go on. We don't know if we'll be on tour after this. I'm not saying he's not a virtuoso ... and that comes from his disability, not being able to play perfectly in time. I'm not a virtuoso either; however, my timing, thankfully, is good. If it wasn't, we'd be in trouble. Adam made it into U2 because of his Afghan coat, those very cool sunglasses, bass guitar and a curly mop of sandy hair. Could he play? I didn't give a shit. He looked great.'

Larry Mullen Jr, in *U2 By U2* (2006).

'For a lot of people, we're either a spiritual band, or a political band, or just a rock band ... But the real truth about U2 lies in the complications.'

Bono, *Time Out* (20 May 1987).

'I don't feel Paul [McGuinness] protects Bono's persona. He's too willing to expose Bono as a nice guy and over-simplify him. You don't see that happen with Prince. Paul likes to believe it's all done with mirrors and wires. He doesn't like to acknowledge the hard work. Instead of saying, "That was hard, Bono had to put himself through hoops to get it," he'll say, "Oh, Bono just wanted to look cool." By saying that, he takes away from Bono. It implies he needs this stuff to look cool.'

Adam Clayton, in Bill Flanagan, *U2 at the End of the World* (1995).

'I actually don't think U2 is in any kind of mood to go quietly. If we get our songs right, I think we could really be very popular.'

Bono, in *U2 By U2* (2006).

What Others Say About U2

They're known the length and breadth of the world, and they dwell in the kind of swish places that most people wouldn't be allowed into, but it doesn't prevent the rich, the famous and the jobbing rock star or three to have an opinion on what makes U2 the kind of band they are. It must be difficult, when you think about it, to be a part of the international music business without at some point bumping into U2, having a quiet (or loud) word with them, and walking away thinking one of several things about them: two of the most obvious being that they're nice blokes or that they're prats.

'The Pest.'
What the White House affectionately calls Bono, *Q's 50 Most Powerful People in Music* (2002).

'Initially I found the individuals in the band quite odd and quite difficult to deal with. Different background, different ideas ... Bono and Edge were the most assured individuals that I've ever come across; they knew exactly where they were going. They were very demanding in their approach and the expectation was very high.'

Steve Iredale, U2 production manager, in Diana Scrimgeour, *U2 Show* (2004).

'Fuck you, Bono.'

Patti Smith, poet/songwriter, at the 1997 Q Awards when, in presenting Smith with the Inspiration Award, Bono said that he would like to take her home to bed.

'Bono, if you still haven't found what you're looking for, look behind the drum kit.'

Boy George, on his crush on Larry Mullen Jr, in B.P. Fallon, *U2 Faraway So Close* (1994).

'Where's Larry? He always runs away from me.'

Boy George, unrequited, at the Q Awards (30 October 2006).

'They're the only real group I've ever met. They realise that intuitively and there is a great loyalty, perhaps because they realise that none of them would have been a musician without the others.'

Brian Eno, *Propaganda* (1991).

'There is nobody to touch them. Nobody comes anywhere near to their stage shows in terms of ambition, risk, danger and being ahead of their time. Television is all about stories: soaps, dramas, news stories, heartbreaks, tragedies, love stories, and U2 encapsulate all of that because their music and their beliefs and the way they present them are fantastic stories ... This is manna from heaven because you are always, always, always – ten times out of ten – going to get a fantastic soundbite out of Bono. You'll get an extremely lucid and intelligent and often controversial point of view from McGuinness. You'll get a heartfelt insight from Edge. You'll get a down-to-earth, gritty, shoot-from-the-hip statement from Adam and Larry ... The problem with U2 is actually getting them to talk about when they're releasing their record and when they're going to tour, because they want to talk about everything else. They're the antithesis of your day-to-day pop band, in that it appears as if the product is bottom of the agenda.'

Malcolm Gerrie, film/television producer, in Diana Scrimgeour, *U2 Show* (2004).

'Bono is everything I hoped David [Byrne] would become.'

Tina Weymouth, former bassist of Talking Heads, in Bill Flanagan, *U2 at the End of the World* (1995).

'He'd do far more good if he preached the gospel of Jesus. God will take care of that Third World country. Get back to your calling, Bono.'

Stephen Baldwin, actor, attacking the U2 front man for his anti-poverty campaigning, *Q* (September 2006).

'Our favourite out of U2? Adam Clayton – he's the one that most looks like he's in the Pet Shop Boys.'

Kaiser Chiefs, *Q* (April 2006).

'I read with interest that U2, comprising Bono and multi-millionaire musician friends, have decided for tax reasons to move their "business empire" out of Ireland. For a person who puts himself forward as a saviour of the poor and the deprived ... Bono might like to behave as the rest of us in this country [Ireland] and pay tax on his earnings ... Perhaps Bono could practise what he preaches and pay tax [in Ireland] to help the poor and deprived of this state.'

Letter to *The Irish Times* (August 2006).

'My first impression of U2 and my lasting impression of U2 was that they were a band in a way very few people are bands now. The music was the result of those four people, not four instruments. It was those four people in particular angles and differences of approach that they brought to the music.'

Brian Eno, in Barry Devlin (director), *The Making of the Unforgettable Fire Video* (1985).

'Bono is highly intelligent, highly articulate ... I think if he was in any walk of life apart from being a rock star – public administration, business – he would be able to mix it anywhere.'

Bertie Ahern, Taoiseach, *Sunday Independent* (12 November 2006).

'The top band then was U2 and we went through them individually – we knew we had a better singer, guitarist, bass player and drummer. Better songs, too.'

Ian Brown, recalling 1986, *Q* (November 2006).

'I've pretty much seen everybody in the band grow up – or maybe grow sideways!'

Daniel Lanois, record producer, in Diana Scrimgeour, *U2 Show* (2004).

'He's not here because he's spearheaded a halfway successful campaign to abolish world poverty. Nor because his band have stayed together four times as long as The Beatles did and rarely put a foot wrong. It's not even because of the amazing lemon. No, the reason Bono polls is that he's the only megastar on terra firma you could still imagine joining down the local boozer for a pint and a setting-the-world-to-rights session.'

NME's 'Heroes' issue, on Bono, who reached number 24 (13 May 2006)

'Bono lives in the face of danger all the time. He is a superior human being. You have to understand that. There's no one I've ever met like him. No one. And he automatically drives you. And he changes you. After you've experienced him, if you don't change, you're numb.'

Jimmy Iovine, chairman of Interscope Records, in Diana Scrimgeour, *U2 Show* (2004).

'Bono is very needy. He needs food for his mind all the time. I think that one of the reasons he may be interested in meeting people like me or Wim Wenders or many of the other artists that are around here is that they give him food. I like that hunger in him because it means that he won't stand still.'

Salman Rushdie, in Bill Flanagan, *U2 at the End of the World* (1995).

'Wow, you've got a great guitar player in your band. Give my regards to The Hedge.'

Brian May, Queen guitarist, to Bono at Live Aid (13 July 1985).

'You've got to have a massive ego to take yourself that seriously. That's why he's an international superstar and I got the Tube down here. Suits me. If that's what goes with the job, I don't want the job. You have to have an ego to get on stage, but that's beyond it. It's mental illness.'

Paul Weller, on seeing Bono on television meeting heads of state, Q (April 2006).

'Adam's actually a really down-to-earth, homey guy. That's his main fight or disadvantage. He loves rock and roll and living the whole rock star thing, but then again he loves planting an oak tree by himself on a sunny Sunday morning.'

Sebastian Clayton, Adam's brother, in Bill Flanagan, U2 at the End of the World (1995).

'When they start building, they are building on something that's already quite big. They build with Everest in mind, but when they get to the top they still feel the need to go higher. I don't think there is any high point for U2.'

Dennis Sheehan, U2 tour manager since 1983, in Diana Scrimgeour, U2 Show (2004).

'I owe U2 a debt of gratitude for the gesture of solidarity and friendship they made by inviting me to join them on stage at Wembley Stadium. Not many novelists ever experience what it's like to face an audience of over 70,000 people – and, fortunately for everyone, I didn't even have to sing.'

Salman Rushdie, The Irish Times (1993), in Pimm Jal de la Parra, U2 Live – a Concert Documentary (1994).

'[Bono] has taken a decision to use his prominence, if you like, to illustrate other issues. He has said that when the light's shining on you, then you can get it turned onto something else ... Some people don't like it, and his motives can be questioned from time to time, but he's tough enough to take that. He's long since made the decision to use his fame to benefit less fortunate people.'

Paul McGuinness, *Hot Press* (4 October 2006).

'A group whose heart is in Dublin, Ireland, whose spirit is with the world, a group that's never had any problem saying how they feel...'

Jack Nicholson, introducing U2 at Live Aid (13 July 1985).

'I'd love to meet him when he's pulled off the world debt thing and offer my congratulations. That would be lovely, wouldn't it? I wonder if he takes a day off from being the Jiminy Cricket of the rock world?'

Jonathan Ross, television presenter, on Bono, *Q* (December 2004).

'U2 always adhered to a very simple principle, which is: they know what U2 is better than anyone else ... They do one thing. They are U2 and they are the custodians of that. And they love it.'

Barry Devlin, director/early producer/member of Horslips, in Diana Scrimgeour, *U2 Show* (2004).

'A lot of his quotes are kind of quirky. He's cool.'

Britney Spears, on Bono, *Q* (November 2006).

'REM don't really care that much if we're the biggest band in the world, but I think U2 does want that to a certain degree. I talked to Larry about it and he said so. You make conscious decisions. I don't think any of their decisions have changed musically where they want to go, but I think it changes how you want to present yourself, and some of us just aren't really interested in that kind of stuff.'

Peter Buck, REM's guitarist, in Bill Flanagan, *U2 at the End of the World* (1995).

'Larry is the man of the people. He's the completely flamboyant, individualistic drummer ... His style is totally unique ... Adam is exactly the same but in a different way. He is the random element in the band, when it comes to the music ... A lot of people give him stick for playing fairly simple parts, but if Adam wasn't there you'd have three other incredible individual musicians on the loose. You've got to have somebody rooting it down ... Edge is the total brains ... He's the one with the most extreme contradiction, because he's level-headed, even-tempered and he appears like the ultimate scientist. And yet he can do the most amazing lyrical, artistic things ... HMV, as we all call him, is inspiration. Bono's one of the few people who just by pushing himself one stage further can inspire ... He'd be the first to say he's not the world's most accomplished musician, but his soul, his emotion, it just comes out and it touches people.'

Flood, record producer, in Diana Scrimgeour, *U2 Show* (2004).

'You're mighty young to write such heavy lyrics.'

B.B. King, blues guitarist, to Bono in the movie *Rattle And Hum* (1988).

'I said to Bob Dylan, "People are going to be playing your songs for thousands of years." He said, "Man, they're going to be listening to your songs too. It's just no one's going to know how to play them..."'

Edge, in *U2 By U2* (2006).

'Spending time with Bono was like eating dinner on a train – feels like you're moving, going somewhere. Bono's got the soul of an ancient poet and you have to be careful around him. He can roar till the earth shakes.'

Bob Dylan, *Chronicles: Volume One* (October 2004).

'He has a willingness to lead, to achieve what his heart tells him, and a belief that nobody should be living in poverty and hopelessness in the world.'

George Bush, on Bono, *Q's 50 Most Powerful People in Music* (2002).

'Why don't you ever take off your sunglasses?'

Joanne Catherall, singer with Human League, on what she would like to ask Bono, *Q* (December 2004).

'They sure don't spend their money on their clothes.'

Frank Sinatra, on stage at Las Vegas, introducing U2 to his audience (2 April 1987).

'Larry is droll and dour. Typically, his comment on the whole ZooTV experience was: "Fucking hell, all these people pay good money to see U2 and all they get is to watch television." ... There's Adam, Larry, Bono and Edge, but there's also U2, and U2 is a separate entity. Each member of the band may have an opinion but there is an umbrella opinion that's more important. More dominant. U2 collectively sense, however they may feel individually about something, if an idea works for U2. They know instinctively what makes the bigger clock tick. You can nuance something the wrong way and a fundamentally good idea ceases to work for them. Or you can push it a little the other way and it's perfect for U2. It takes U2, the band, to know the answer to that question.'

Kevin Godley, film director/contributor to ZooTV, in Diana Scrimgeour, *U2 Show* (2004).

'I'm surprised Bono can still talk, his mouth is so full of American politician cock.'

Sinead O'Connor, *Q* (January 2006). Bono's response: 'A mouth full of cock is a tough charge but I can't say I've never felt that myself sometimes.'

'Bono, the Mother Teresa of abandoned songs, compassionately argues for every single idea that has ever experienced even the most transitory existence. Larry and Adam are reliable wide-anglers when things start to lose perspective or become too narrowly focused. They become the voice of musical conscience. Edge, the archaeologist of the rough mix, delves back through earlier strata in the song's development, emerging triumphantly with a different version on a battered cassette.'

Brian Eno, *Rolling Stone* (28 November 1991).

'They take chances, they take risks and they're not afraid of falling flat on their faces.'

Salman Rushdie, on why he likes U2, in B.P. Fallon, *U2 Faraway So Close* (1994).

'When they went up to collect their 'Best U2 Award', he had a whole poem prepared. It's not Beat night – you're

supposed to go, "Love you Mum, bye", and then get off ...
Bono might as well have got the scrolls of The Torah out, he's
so self-important.'

Amy Winehouse, at the Q Awards, *Hot Press Yearbook*
(2006).

'Paul always used to draw these bizarre pictures of guys lying
down with their tongues hanging out, and with nails through
the tongues. Quite weird.'

Chris de Burgh, recalling Paul McGuinness' editorship of
Trinity College's student magazine *TCD Miscellany*, in *Chris
de Burgh – the Authorised Biography* (1996).

'It was very straightforward. If they said they were going to
do something, that's what they did. If they said they weren't
going to do something, then you might as well stop debating
it. If they said they were going to send you a cheque, they
sent you a cheque. There was never any messing around ...'

Jeremy Thom, U2 set designer on The Joshua Tree tour, in
Diana Scrimgeour, *U2 Show* (2004).

'Everyone gets the same. Why should he get anything
special? He's paying the same price. It's not like he's the
singer in Whitesnake, is it?'

Marco Pierre White, chef, on being asked whether Bono
might receive preferential treatment if he walked into one of
his restaurants, *Q* (February 2007).

'In every performance that I've seen them do, what comes
across with the band is a passion and the fact that it's just
four guys on stage. It's still the four guys. That, to me, is what
U2 is about. They are that group in the true sense of the

word. It is the four of them taking on the world, and Paul there behind them pushing them up that hill.'

Denis Desmond, Irish-based concert promoter, in Diana Scrimgeour, *U2 Show* (2004).

'They haven't been very honest about where their influences have come from, have they? A great deal of U2 has to do with early P.I.L. It's the Edge all over, isn't it? That's fine, that's not an insult. He liked it and he took it to someplace else. Made it his own. Well, good luck to him. It just gets irritating when people tell me, "Oh, you're not as good as U2." Don't you know where they came from?'

John Lydon, former lead singer of The Sex Pistols and P.I.L., in Bill Flanagan, *U2 at the End of the World* (1995).

Image

Image problems? They've had a few. In the beginning, of course, they had no image at all; they were just another ambitious urban post-punk band (if that) with no sense of style and a puzzling sense of purpose. *The Joshua Tree* and *Rattle And Hum* years saw them adopt a distinctly American image of immigrant Preacher Man, but that was ditched in the lead up to perhaps their greatest (and highly calculated) image change of all: as sexy, witty, irony-snagging rock stars *circa Achtung Baby, Zooropa* and *Pop.* As they entered their forties, image seemed to become less important to them, and they latterly resemble not so much a working rock band at the top of their game, but rather a group of quite mature men that look (Larry excepting – as the drummer he will always sweat too much) as if they'd rather choose clothes from Commes de Garçon than Topshop.

'Getting the name 'U2' right visually was quite important. Our earliest attempt to do that was a construction made out of red plastic drainpipes spelling out 'U2'. We used to erect that at the back of the stage I think even before we had a record deal, and try to get people to recognise that U2 were on the stage. There's an old photograph from the Dandelion Market where we have a banner behind the band saying 'U2'. That was our earliest attempt at establishing an identity, otherwise nobody knew who it was.'

Paul McGuinness, in Diana Scrimgeour, *U2 Show* (2004).

Interviewer: 'What's the most frightening thing that ever happened to you?'

Bono: 'I found this pair of sunglasses, I picked them up, I put them on...'

Bono, *ZooTV Tour Programme* (1992).

'Though it's difficult to imagine the rather serious-looking characters who adorned *The Joshua Tree*'s stark, monochrome sleeve impersonating The Village People and preaching kitsch, U2, like Bowie, found that radical reinvention can help sustain a legend.'

James McNair, *Mojo* (December 1998).

'It really started with 'The Fly', Bono writing that lyric from the point of view of a different character. He had never explored irony before, or the freedom that comes in writing about something serious in an indirect or apparently flippant way. The junk shop shades gave him a clue to a whole different persona ... That playful aspect of U2 had been lost. I think we were drawn to anything that was going to give us a chance to get away from *The Joshua Tree* earnestness, which had become so stifling ... No one knew we had a sense of humour, we had become glum rock's leading lights. ZooTV ... finally killed off the old idea that we were a band of painfully earnest people who didn't know how to have a good time.'

Edge, in *U2 By U2* (2006).

'I see pictures of myself and think, Oh God. I can look like a rock star. But I can also look like a pudgy politician. Or a darts player. It's always sexy on the inside, though.'

Bono, *Q* (November 2004).

'I once met an American tourist in Ireland who said she had been having tea in a hotel restaurant when U2 came in and sat at the table behind her. She and her friend could not believe how funny the four of them were – they traded jokes, quips and can-you-top-this punchlines. "They were like a comedy team," she said. "I always thought they were serious."'

Bill Flanagan, *Propaganda* (1993).

'I had no idea about videos, none of us did. I had just bought a brand new pair of red Doc Martens boots, which cost me fifteen pounds, a lot of money back then. There was a scene where the director, Meiert Avis, asked me to splash through a puddle. I said, "I'll get my new Docs wet." He said, "Yeah, well that's what we want for the scene." I told him, "Forget it." I wasn't getting the boots wet.'

Larry Mullen Jr, on the making of the video for 'Gloria', in *U2 By U2* (2006).

'Still the most famous image of U2.'

Anton Corbijn, photographer, on the cover of *The Joshua Tree*, *Q* (August 2006).

'I had one of the worst haircuts of the 1980s. I know that it launched a million second-division soccer players. But the truth of it, if I'm really honest, is that I thought I looked like David Bowie.'

Bono, on his 1980s bad-hair days, *Q* (August 2006).

'Bono has always played with the notion of character in his performances: he comes across as the cowboy or the Devil or the boxing champ – and all of these characters might be said to be comments on his role as an artist and a vocalist. It is a game with identity which has appealed to artists as different in style as Jeff Koons, Cindy Sherman and Gavin Turk. It seems to replicate a comment by Marcel Proust, where he writes of the many gentlemen of whom he is comprised. And Bono, through the medium of U2, can not only play the roles of those different gentlemen, but frame the performances with the most spectacular and self-analytical of settings.'

Michael Bracewell, journalist and author, in Diana Scrimgeour, *U2 Show* (2004).

'We suffered a bit from that [image] in the 1980s because U2 became a caricature, partly our fault I must admit. But we didn't have the slightest idea of the danger that could lead to. That's why we decided to change strategy [for *Achtung Baby*], so that the greatest possible confusion reigns, making it synonymous with originality and erasing the caricatures which have been made around the group.'

Bono, *Propaganda* (1992).

The early mistakes we made – not understanding cool, not understanding attitude, clothes, haircuts – were because we were seventeen and eighteen and our idols were like The

Clash and The Jam and The Police, who had all that shit down ... They had their image together. It's taken us fifteen years to get an image together, or indeed to realise that image is important. And not important.'

Adam Clayton, in Bill Flanagan, *U2 at the End of the World* (1995).

'We don't have any style ... Swagger, but no style.'

Bono, *Achtung Baby: the Videos, the Cameos and a Whole Lot of Interference from ZooTV* (1992).

'For quite a while, we sort of defined ourselves in contrast to all those early 1980s British groups who only had irony, who hid behind a wink. That whole thing of clever-clever lyrics at the expense of soul. I've always preferred Van Morrison or Bob Marley, to be quite honest. But, in retrospect, I think we followed that idea through to the end ... I guess the big difference is now we've discovered that irony is not necessarily the enemy of the soul.'

Edge, *Details* (September 1992).

'It's kind of weird that the way you look is about as important as the way you sound.'

Larry Mullen Jr, in *U2 By U2* (2006).

'The sense of humour of this band is missed a lot. It's like some American papers reported that we had done a Save The Yuppie concert – the same band who did concerts for human rights and for the starving peoples of Africa were very concerned about the Crash ... It was reported without irony. It was like the time lightning hit the airplane when we were flying into America, and we were sitting opposite Sophia

Loren and I said, "Don't worry, it's only God taking your photograph" and she laughed. And then the story came out in a very serious way. It's just one of those things. Maybe people don't expect us to have a sense of humour so they don't look for a sense of humour in anything we do.'

Bono, *Hot Press* (December 1988).

'It's the moment I actually meet the people that enjoy our music that's very special. We cannot control what people think of us, [but] when we meet people, we just underline the fact that we are the same as they are. We may be in a privileged position in a creative field of music, but other than that there's essentially no difference.'

Edge, radio interview with Carter Alan, on Boston's WBCN (1983).

'It's always pleasant to work with [U2] … They like to look good, like anyone else, but for public images they don't like to be jokey either. We take quite a lot of photos where they are laughing but they don't get published – except occasionally.'

Anton Corbjin, photographer, *Propaganda* (1989).

'The distorting lens that is fame makes people ugly and self-conscious. The lips drain of blood, the face is suddenly harrowed. The photograph is being taken, but the reason why you wanted to take the photograph is gone. In the 1980s, I was that. I thought about it too much.'

Bono on Bono (2005).

'Yes. Provided my bits were looking good. I'm not sure whether it's something I'd like to do past the age of … fifty-five. But I think there should be more male nudes. Men should be encouraged to look at each other's bits. Penises, I'm inclined to believe – and I'm not just talking about my own – are good things. They needn't be hidden under a bushel.'

Adam Clayton, on being asked would he ever pose naked again on a U2 album cover – he bared all on the cover of *Achtung Baby*, *Q* (November 2000).

'He's very easy with himself. It was a lot easier for him to do that than it was for me, actually. That particular way of shooting requires you to be very close to the body. It's to do with accumulation of light. So I had to kneel down in front of him. I was very close to ... everything.'

Anton Corbijn, photographer, on shooting Adam Clayton naked, *Irish Times Magazine* (25 August 2001).

'Early on, we thought that we were making a non-statement, that our style was an "anti-style style". What we didn't realise is that that was a style anyway.'

The Edge, in *U2 By U2* (2006).

'Safe.'

Bono, on being asked how he felt the first time he put on his Fly shades, *Q* (November 2006).

'Maybe over our career, our ability to create music that shows the full range of the personalities of Bono and the other members of the band was very poor. But that's the truth – that guy is totally different to the way most people think of him. He's far funnier, takes himself far less seriously than most people think. He's wild, he's not reserved. None of the clichés that spring to mind when you think of people's perception of him. This is not just a problem for Bono, this is a problem for the whole band. Everyone has this sort of caricature impression of what we are like.'

Edge, in Bill Flanagan, *U2 at the End of the World* (1995).

'Everything I say becomes some sort of statement, something of vast importance. I could go on stage, unzip my pants, and hang my dick out and people would think it was some statement about something.'

Bono, *Spin* (January 1989).

'Very interested' (Adam). 'Easily bored but easy to take' (Larry). 'Always looks the same ...' (Edge). 'Quite hard to photograph because he has so many different faces but is therefore my favourite' (Bono).

Anton Corbjin, photographer, on sessions with U2, *Propaganda* (1989).

'We shot the session as they were travelling through the airport, there were no poses, it was very spontaneous.'

Steve Averill, designer, on the cover of *All That You Can't Leave Behind*, *Irish Times Magazine* (25 August 2001).

'The whole Fly thing, Bono with the glasses. People were really bothered by the glasses. Gone was the forthright persona, and in its place was irony, the last thing their audience expected from U2. The audience perceived a change in their accessibility and some resented it. I also think it marked a change in Bono. Probably it was just self-preservation, a decision not to give quite so much of himself away. Of course, it was partly parodying the whole celebrity thing, but I think it was also his way of acknowledging that he needed some cover. *The Joshua Tree* was just heart on your sleeve, right out there, giving it all away, all the time. This was different. We'd go into interview situations, and people would want him to take his glasses off, which he would refuse to do. It was a shtick. But I also think he started to need the distance they created ... I think their audience loved their openness, but you can just end up with nothing for yourself.'

Ellen Darst, Principle Management employee 1983–93, in Diana Scrimgeour, *U2 Show* (2004).

'Relieved at first, and then I realised everyone was going to know what a great bunch of guys he was.'

Larry, on being asked how he felt the first time Bono put on the Fly shades, *Q* (November 2006).

'I realised we were in trouble when Paramount showed me the 12-foot-high poster of me with my stubble airbrushed out. I just went, "Oh, shit, we really got this one wrong." But by then it was too late.'

Edge, on the transformation of *Rattle And Hum* from a little road movie into a Hollywood production, *Vanity Fair* (November 2004).

'When we first met Phil Joanou [director of *Rattle And Hum*] he promised faithfully that he'd make us all look like Montgomery Clift in his heyday. He turned out to be a lying bastard (laughs), so we were all very shocked when we saw we looked like Bono, Larry, Adam and Edge, and we were very, very upset. What I'm really trying to say is that we could have gone like Hollywood and got all the real expensive lights and made ourselves look amazing, but this film was being shot to try and capture the way it really is. Warts and all.'

Edge, *Hot Press* (October 1988).

'It was tricky getting Larry into the Village People gag. But he's comfortable and amused by his gay icon status and almost ready to laugh at all of this. The emphasis being on "almost".'

Bono, in *U2 By U2* (2006).

'We may almost have become the photographs. We became as severe as Anton's images.'

Bono, on the iconic images of U2 on *The Joshua Tree* album, *Q* (January 1993).

'It's so important for us that we climb down from this past decade of artifice in the presentation of the material. There's never any artifice in the material itself – it's always been the same for us. The irony is, there's no irony in those songs on *Achtung Baby*, *Zooropa* and *Pop* … Nellee Hooper came up to me at a party recently and said, "Irony, you've ruined it for everybody."'

Bono, *Q* (July 2001).

'Many of the gay community [in San Francisco] believed that the boy on the cover [of debut album, *Boy*] had some gay connotations, and that the little boy was me. So when we went to San Francisco there was quite a bit of heat on me. I was seriously wigged out. It was very hard to be comfortable with that kind of attention. My first reaction was to be very pissed off. I was being described as a gay icon. "What's that?" Eventually, I woke up and thought: That's brilliant. I'm really flattered.'

Larry Mullen Jr, in *U2 By U2* (2006).

'*Achtung Baby* is definitely a reaction to the myth of U2. We never really had any control over that myth. You could say we helped it along a bit, but the actual myth itself is a creation of the media and people's imagination. Like all myths. There is very little resemblance to the actual personalities of the band or the intentions of the band, and *Achtung Baby* balances things out a bit.'

Edge, in Bill Flanagan, *U2 at the End of the World* (1995).

Fashion

Fashion is something that always goes out of style, which is why we are, to all intents and purposes, victims of it. U2 have always tried to make their albums quite different from each other. This is one of the reasons why their music has (in our opinion, that is) never really sounded stale or dated, and the main reason why over the past twenty or so years, U2 have managed the incredible trick of never really being out of fashion. Out of favour, perhaps, but more often than not always in the zone of popular culture, right in the centre of what's happening, in thrall to their heroes (Bob Dylan, Leonard Cohen, Lou Reed, Patti Smith, The Who, etc.) as much as newish bands (The Killers, Coldplay, Snow Patrol, Arcade Fire, etc.) are in thrall to them. As these things go, that's no small achievement.

'Rock 'n' roll has always been visual. When Elvis moved his hips that was the visual representation of that music. And out of that there came a youth culture that existed probably up until the end of the 1980s, where everyone was forced to be young and have their hair dyed blond and wear blue jeans and white T-shirts. As long as they looked young, they were hip. I think we've broken that barrier. I think we accept knowledge now and we accept that you can be as hip at fifty as you can at fifteen, probably more so.'

Adam Clayton, *PopMart Tour Programme* (1997).

Bono: 'I was never ready-made to be a rock star: a brickie, a boxer or at the very least a bouncer. Actually, darts player is more like it, certainly if I've been off tour and not in the gym. All attempts at flamboyance have backfired. Nowadays I stick to jeans and T-shirt ... I love suits, bespoke or Helmut Lang ...'

Edge: '1989's raggle-taggle Lovetown [tour] look reflected my state of mind at the time – all over the place.'

Adam: 'In hindsight some might suggest the surgical mask during PopMart [1997/98] was a mistake.'

Larry: 'N/A.'

On being asked what their biggest fashion disaster was, *Q* (November 2006).

'Even in a frock I look like Fred Flintstone.'
Bono on Bono (2005).

'U2 have had two really rotten fashion phases. One was the October tour, where I had a skunk on my head. It looked like a badger, actually; early experiments with peroxide, and it didn't work ... The second was the *Unforgettable Fire* period. That was pretty rough because I'd taken to wearing military boots that were knee high. You should never draw attention to your legs if you don't have any. And forget about having a bad hair day, I was having a bad hair life. You should never look like you've had your hair ironed. I look at pictures from that period and I am the Prince of Mullet, and the only thing that's keeping that mullet away from pop history is a hat designed for a taller man. There's still people who can't like us because of that hair-do.'

Bono, in *U2 By U2* (2006).

'You invented Britney. Where would she have been without the midriff?'

Adam Clayton, on Larry's first photo shoot, *Q* (January 2007).

'Bono with chequerboard pants and polo-necks with one nipple cut out. That was probably the silliest it got.'

Edge, on those early fashion mistakes, in *U2 By U2* (2006).

Pretentious? Moi?

No, they're not always down to earth, as you might presume from their backgrounds. And it seems that, occasionally, they get ideas above their elevated station. And yes, mostly it's Bono who comes out with some risible pearls of wisdom. But, then, we've all had a few too many glasses of shandy, haven't we? And said some very silly things as the bubbles float to our head. And, yes, they'll probably never live down the giant lemon (now that's a stage prop) that once refused to open. But was that pretension writ large? Or was it a good idea that just didn't work? And speaking of which – where exactly are the bones of MacPhisto resting?

'I was always concerned that the further we moved from what we knew, the greater the danger we'd disappear up our own arses. I couldn't cope with being called a pretentious prat.'

Larry Mullen Jr, on U2 and their 'irony' period, *Q* (November 2004).

'You put your hand in under your skin, you break your breastbone, you rip open your rib cage ... Are you ready to do that? Or is rock 'n' roll for you just a pair of shoes and a haircut, or a certain sour existentialism or a certain sweet decay? That was one of my first definitions of art. Blood ... In Ireland, that pain of opening your rib cage, it's in us.'

Bono on Bono (2005).

'I'm not sure what the thrill is of watching Bono. I think it must be something along the lines of the way you might watch one of those guys who jumps off tall buildings in New York with a few plastic bags as parachutes. It's a slightly will-he-or-won't-he thrill.'

Bono, *Q* (July 2002).

'To make a recognisable image of Bono's outward appearance while attempting to portray the wavelength of his inner dynamism.'

The Irish Development Authority, in a pitch about Louis Le Brocquy's painting of Bono's head, *The Irish Times* (15 November 2006).

'A crappier and more, well, insulting record would be hard to imagine. Bono's mumbling take on 'I Got You Under My Skin' confirms his covetable status as World's Most Pretentious Human Being.'

Review of Frank Sinatra's album *Duets*, *NME* (November 1993).

Confessional

U2 as an entity have, through the many years of their life, been beaten around, about and on by a big thick stick. These occasional bouts of violence have been brought on by the band, collectively and individually, being upfront and honest about things that are important to them: love, life, family, people, the human spirit, the Holy Ghost, sex, death, taxes and music. Ultimately, what the band are saying is as simple as this: whether you agree with us or not, take us as we are. Of course, confessionals come in all sorts of shapes and sizes: stark, subtle, agonising, funny, heartfelt. So, U2: take them as they are. They won't care if you don't like them. Really.

'The right to be stupid and irresponsible is something I hold very dear. And luckily it's something I do very well. It's always confused people – quoting scriptures and then swearing at them. But you have to be who you are.'

Bono, *Q* (July 2001).

'I do see the good in people, but I also see the bad – I see it in myself. I know what I'm capable of, good and bad. It's very important that we make that clear. Just because I often find a way around the darkness doesn't mean that I don't know it's there.'

Bono on Bono (2005).

'I don't like meetings. You have to be a sort of businessman at this stage and sign cheques and all that sort of stuff, and I hate that side of it. Have the meetings in the pub!'

Adam Clayton, *Propaganda* (1989).

'All my mates were intent on going to college and on doing things. I'd always been bright at school and the last thing I wanted was to stay stuck in any kind of rut. Joining the band was my emancipation from all this. It was my ticket to freedom. It was my way of attempting to change the circumstances I was living in.'

Bono, in Niall Stokes, *Into the Heart: The Stories behind Every U2 Song* (2001).

'I just want to be able to walk into a pub, have somebody buy me a drink and sit down and have a chat – because that's the hardest thing in the world to achieve. It's really that simple.'

Adam Clayton, *Propaganda* (1989).

'I feel at home in chaos.'

Bono, *Propaganda* (1987).

'I am able to write, always, because as a writer I am always unable not to be true. As a performer it isn't always so. You know the thing that keeps me honest as a performer? The fucking high notes I have to sing. Because unless I am totally in that character, I actually can't sing – it's out of my range. That's what keeps me honest on a stage.'

Bono on Bono (2005).

'My drumming career has always been based on a complete lack of expertise.'

Larry Mullen Jr, *Rhythm Magazine* (1993).

'I was holding onto the record [*Rattle And Hum*] as a kind of lifeline. I was going under, personally, and my marriage was disappearing up in smoke very fast ... I threw myself into the record and that probably didn't help the situation at home. I think Aislinn felt abandoned because I was so completely caught up with what I was doing that I wasn't there in any kind of meaningful way. We're not talking about a small road bump, we're talking about fundamental problems that probably had always been lurking, and just being in the pressure cooker of the music business and the success we'd had, it all unravelled spectacularly.'

Edge, in *U2 By U2* (2006).

'I need to be surrounded, even just for the laughter, because if I run out of laughs, then I'm really in trouble.'

Bono on Bono (2005).

'If you had said to this twenty-one year old [Bono] that one day he's gonna be on the cover of *Time* magazine he probably would have believed you. That's puberty for you – it was late in my case. But the other things in my life ... Family, I'd say, he would have approved of. But the complications, the hesitations, the drinking, the well-to-do lifestyle – he would have been a bit hard on me on that one. Because he was a bit of a zealot.'

Bono on Bono (2005).

'I don't think I was destined for any kind of greatness in my life before U2. The best decision I ever made was to be part of U2 and I guess I haven't needed to make another serious decision since then.'

Adam Clayton, in *U2 By U2* (2006).

'You want your family to be proud of you. I have nightmares of my kids saying, "Did you really look like that? Did you really make that shit?" I want to make good enough records for them to be able to say I'm OK.'

Larry Mullen Jr, *Q* (July 2001).

'I have to fight harder for fitness. I can't drink the same amounts. I can't eat the same amounts. I don't stay on for as long as I used to. I'm not afraid of that. On death, I fear other people's. I would miss my friends.'

Bono on Bono (2005).

'It was a difficult decision to get to, because so much of what I thought being creative and being relevant was about, was staying up late, having a good time and living it large. But I got to the point where I realised that it didn't suit me anymore. I wasn't any good at it. I wasn't living a particularly musical life, I was living a more isolated life. I was paranoid, uncomfortable. It was very hard being in that place of really facing yourself and overcoming layers of denial. But I'm very happy with the way things turned out.'

Adam Clayton, on quitting alcohol, *Q* (November 2000).

'I buy socks ... I'm still the kind of rich that likes a familiar pair of socks.'

Adam Clayton, on being asked what he spends money on instead of alcohol, *Q* (November 2000).

'Confidence gets you not very far in this life. But for me, it's a sure sign of pure panic.'

Bono on Bono (2005).

'I have a curiosity which compels me to want to find ways to make music that are fresh and new, and I have the focus to keep going until we realise our goals. If Bono should be attending Over-Achievers Anonymous, I might have to take the twelve steps to Workaholics Anonymous.'

Edge, in *U2 By U2* (2006).

'If I knew who I was, I wouldn't be an artist. I wouldn't be in a band. I wouldn't be here screaming for a living.'

Bono, *Q* (June 1995).

'I have a few blind spots, but one of them is I don't sometimes see obstacles.'

Bono on Bono (2005).

'I need them for when I'm being insincere ...'

Bono, on the subject of his shades, *Q* (February 1998).

'I'm always looking for clues. Some people have them and some people don't have any. When people don't have any clues, I'm less likely to stick around. I don't in any way consider myself to be above anybody else, but I'm just excited when I'm in the company of older people, because they have so much more to offer. Sitting there with some punk rocker who's just figured how to look good in the mirror is not really on to keep me up.'

Bono on Bono (2005).

'Dick was a scientist, and I didn't understand why we had a scientist in the band. I was young and naïve and not very diplomatic. Sorry, Dick.'

Larry Mullen Jr, finally apologising to Edge's brother for vetoing his membership in an early incarnation of the band, in *U2 By U2* (2006).

'In the 1980s I thought too much about being famous. Ali sat me down and said, "The man I fell in love with had mischief in his eyes. He had fun and he laughed. Where is he?" And I think I had gone somewhere, possibly where the sun doesn't shine.'

Bono, *Q* (January 2006).

'Most mornings, now, I really don't think about being in a band. I think about being a father, I think about being a husband, I think about being a friend.'

Bono on Bono (2005).

'My mother's death in a road-traffic accident in November 1978 was, in the end, what made my mind up with regard to the band. I am not saying I wouldn't have jumped had she lived but, after her death, there was nowhere else I wanted to be.'

Larry Mullen Jr, in *U2 By U2* (2006).

'I had a bit of a fright ... It can happen to you even if you don't have a scare. Suddenly your mortality walks into the room. You feel immortal when you're sixteen, you want to drive the car as fast as you can, and then there comes a moment in your life when you don't want to crash because you ... you ... love it. I just realised that I really like being alive.'

Bono, on health worries, *Q* (July 2001).

'There's a noise that you see on the surface, a kind of certain frenetic hyperactive person doing lots of things, with lots of interests and ideas that I'm chasing. But below that, really, at the very bottom of that, there is peace. I feel, when I'm on my own, a peace that's hard to describe, a peace that passes all understanding. Some people look really calm on the outside and serene, but deep down they are cauldrons. They are boiling with nervous energy. All my nervous energy's on the outside. On the inside there is calm.'

Bono on Bono (2005).

'Naomi [Campbell] came to a show and we met ... That relationship brought with it the dubious pleasures of the paparazzi. On the one hand that can be a lot of fun and not to be taken too seriously, but it can be a little invasive as well. Despite being in a world famous rock band, I'm not someone who particularly lives in public. I think there are people who do and they can manage it and it's no great difficulty for them, but it was a difficulty for me ... This was not a good time for me. I was heading for a crash, everything was spinning out of control. I definitely wasn't prepared for it and I wasn't really able to deal with everything that came with Naomi ... All I can say is that in the end it didn't work for me and that's a wisdom I've acquired in retrospect. When I look back now and look at what went wrong, it wasn't the right place for me. But you don't know that until you try it.'

Adam Clayton, in *U2 By U2* (2006).

'You know, it's no surprise to me how ugly the world can be, but I have to remind myself to pay attention to how beautiful it can be. To see a wave crashing in. Or a beautiful tree. Or a beach full of breasts, heh heh.'

Bono, *Q* (November 2000).

'I remember the last thing he said to me. I was sitting at the side of his bed and he woke with a start. I asked him if he was okay and his mouth started moving. By then all he could do was whisper. I had to put my ear to his mouth. And he said, "Fuck off!" Then he said, "This place is a prison. Take me home."'

Bono, at his father's death bed, *Q* (November 2004).

'It's the sort of loneliness a spoilt brat has that's been put outside the door. We've got this small town on the road and I love a lot of these people and I think each and every one of them would let me in if I knocked on their door. That's not loneliness, is it?'

Bono, in B.P. Fallon, *U2 Faraway So Close* (1994).

'I don't have many memories from my early life. I've talked about this with my brother because he doesn't have many either. The only explanation we can come up with is that when my mother died, my father didn't talk about her, at all, ever. So as a result of her being erased from memory, simply through not wanting to go there, I think a lot of other stuff went with her. It's a real singer's thing, missing mothers ... It seems to be the very heart of rock 'n' roll.'

Bono, in *U2 By U2* (2006).

'There is nothing like a brush with mortality to put things into perspective. Everything comes into sharper focus, you really appreciate what you might have lost ... If you think you may not be able to sing again, well, then you're not going to mess around.'

Bono, on his cancer scare in the early-2000s, in *U2 By U2* (2006).

Interviewer: 'What's the most frightening thing that ever happened to you?'

Edge: 'Breaking up with my wife.'

Edge, *ZooTV Tour Programme* (1992).

'Bono's relationship with his father was complicated and never easy. They were very alike. Although he would never say it, I think his father was enormously proud of Bono. I don't know why he couldn't tell him.'

Paul McGuinness, in *U2 By U2* (2006).

'Hello, my name's Cheryl, and last week I 'ad sex on the back of an 'Arley Davidson. It was fuckin' fantastic.'

One of the many confessionals on ZooTV's Video Confessional Box.

Acknowledgements

I would like to thank the following for their help and assistance in the piecing together of this book: Eoghan Corry for his initial advice, Hodder Headline Ireland for their enthusiasm for the project, HHI editor Claire Rourke for diligently overseeing the work and for not harrassing me over deadlines, and agent Chelsey Fox for taking care of business.

Every book takes time to put together, particularly something as research-heavy as this one, so in that regard I'd like to pay due respect to all the magazines and books I browsed through, and all the writers and authors whose work I filleted for quotes. I'd also like to thank my family for having the grace to give me the time to work on something like this – without their support it just wouldn't have been started, let alone embarked upon.

Tony Clayton-Lea
April 2007